PETE'S SAKE

The life and wisdom of
an honorable man

NINA CICALE

Pete's Sake
Nina Cicale
All of Us Publishing Florida
United States of America

Library of Congress Cataloging
Cicale, Nina
Pete's Sake/Nina Cicale
ISBN 978-0-9854483-1-8
Non fiction
Biography
Cultural heritage
Memoir
Self help

In memory of our parents

Peter and Catherine Cicale

Jack and Mickie Zucker

With love

And a special legacy for our

little ones,

Skylar, Peyton,

Eathan, Tavin, Gabriel, Maya

Contents

Acknowledgments

I would like to acknowledge the main contributor for this amazing journey, my husband, Gabriel. Without his belief in me, Pete's life story would have been impossible to write.

I wish to thank all family members of the Cicale and Porpiglia family for their memories, patience, and their guidance in telling me stories and family history.

I wish to thank the many people of the Hudson Valley for their history lessons.

Special thanks to Cliff Carle, my editor and mentor for the encouragement and the lessons.

Thank you to Jason Alexander for the difficult task of coordinating the pictures.

My beautiful picture was taken by talented photographer Neal Bredbeck.

Warm thanks for my cover design by artist Gregory Doroshenko, his help in formatting this book, and his wonderful wife Helen for her invaluable expertise.

My sincerest appreciation to Valencia Jackson Coley who has worked with me for so many years, can read my mind, and take over wherever I have shortcomings. Her artistic talent and creativity have helped me greatly. She is also responsible for my outstanding website.

Finally, I want to thank Peter and Catherine Cicale who have taught me how to live my life with dignity and honor.

Author's Note

This book is the life story of Peter Cicale, the father of my husband.

I have done my best to achieve accuracy wherever possible. But, as with all books about the past, I have had to improvise in certain places where the information was not related first hand.

This does not take away from my father-in-law, the true hero of our story.

Prologue
A MEETING

It was late summer in the small park. Daylight was slowly descending. The elder man looked as though he'd put on his clothing in the dark; a rumpled well worn checkered shirt, a pair of plaid Bermuda shorts with dark shoes and yellow socks. Nothing matched. The younger man who approached him was from a different place and time, dressed to the nines, as if he'd made a left turn on Wall Street and ended up lost in this park. His entire outfit showed money; his custom navy blue double breasted suit, pale blue and yellow checked shirt, an expensive yellow and blue handmade patterned tie, his brown alligator shoes shined to reflect off the setting sun, an expensive haircut and of course the prerequisite tan. The waning sun beamed down on the rugged strong face of the elder of the two, eyes glowing, and a warm serene smile.

The elder was the caretaker, the park superintendent, of this little piece of heaven, completely at peace in his surroundings, spending twelve hours a day walking the park, cleaning and greeting all of his friends, from the small kids to the elderly, just like himself. His name was Pete, a simple name and all ages referred to him in the same way: "Hi, Pete." And he would let loose that infectious smile, as he returned the greeting, knowing everyone by name. After all, he was the king of his present day world.

To an independent observer, it might have appeared that the younger man was there to aid the elderly gentleman, but in fact he was concentrating heavily as the older man spoke to him.

He paused, reached into his pocket and pulled out a crumpled bill, smoothed it out and held it up to his son. "Remember Bill, son? Dollar Bill? When you have the dollar bill in your pocket you have lots of friends. When you do not have Bill, then see where your friends are."

The younger man smiled back and nodded to his father. "Yes, Dad, I remember."

This was one of the many gems that the older man had taught him throughout his life. It was the philosophy the elder lived by; his code of life, that he would use for himself, his family, friends, the common man like himself. Even the CEOs of large corporations who lived in this small hamlet in the Hudson Valley of New York, occasionally came to him for advice. It made no difference who spoke with this man; he was so comfortable in his own skin. He knew that money was every man's barometer. He just didn't want it to be his. He had lived his life following the same adages that gave him a satisfying life; one measured by living honorably, according to his code of ethics. His son calls them "Peteisms" his father's lessons on life.

The two sat together on a bench reminiscing. When the conversation lulled, the elder looked off into the distance, gazing off to another time and place. Pete, born In New York City in 1905, remembered all the way back to being very young, circa 1912.

Picture a quieter world, with horse drawn carriages, push carts, open windows, clothes lines, and the streets filled with all nationalities, who have come so far to have their shot at the American dream. A seven-year-old boy dressed in knickers and a slosh hat carries his shoe shine kit to his corner on 117th Street and Pleasant Avenue on the upper east side of New York, which in today's time would be known as Harlem. He charged five cents a shine, bringing home five dollars a week to feed his eight brothers and sisters, father and mother. Why him? Pete just stepped up to the plate, when his father did not. He always knew that his mother depended on him and he was wise, way beyond his years.

He was the fourth child of Italian immigrants all born within eighteen years, approximately two years apart. Pete never asked what he could do, he just did it. As he grew, he graduated to more difficult jobs. When he was eight, he carried sixty pound blocks of ice up many flights of stairs in the tenement buildings, which would be put on the top of the ice boxes to keep food cold for a week. Refrigerators were starting to appear throughout the country, but not to these people. They could never have afforded one.

By the time he was nine, Pete was working on the laundry wagon. The poor women of the tenements would send their laundry out dry and dirty and the clothing would be returned clean and damp, weighing up to one hundred pounds. Little Pete would then have to carry or drag the wet laundry up the four or five flights of stairs to deliver to all the families. There were no washing machines or dryers for the people, hence the clothes lines hung from building to building with shirts, pants, dresses, sheets, underwear, socks; all creating a coat of many colors above the sidewalks of New York.

Pete continued to help his mom until her death, always feeling an obligation to support her. When Pete turned thirty-four, he married and had his children. Pete never complained. He was with the same woman his father and his wife's father had decided he should marry. They were together for forty-six years and raised three children in a home that Pete had built himself.

At the end of his life when he was given last rites for the second and final time in his life, he was asked only three questions. The first question put forth by the priest was, "Are you ready to leave this life?"

Pete responded, "Yes."

The second question was, "Do you regret anything in your life?"

Pete calmly responded, "No."

The priest asked his third and final question: "Is there anything you feel you would like to say?"

Pete's response was simply this: "No, I have done what I came to earth for and am now content and ready to go."

This man, who had lived his life so unpretentiously, chose to die the same way. The priest was so taken by Pete and his answers that he wrote a special letter to my mother saying that in all his years in the priesthood he had never met a man so strong in his conviction, and ready to die with a smile on his face.

My dad died the way he lived, without any fanfare never drawing attention. To him, it was inevitable; just another phase in life's cycle.

It is difficult to understand why this child was the one to "bring home the bacon", but Pete believed he was an old soul, who knew that responsibility was an honor, and not to be taken lightly. He managed to go through seven grades in school, but survival of the family came first; he knew that as he grew, so did his ability to work harder, and so he did. What makes Pete unique among men was that he instinctively knew his role in life.

Pete was a man of few words but wiser than any man I've ever known. He had limited formal schooling, but Pete had a PhD in life. His story unfolds to teach us that there are no guessing games in survival, just his simple one liners, his *Peteisms*, passing on his wisdom to all that chose to listen. They are more apropos now than ever before in a world that is moving so rapidly forward, only to stop us in our tracks, to teach us that we must learn the fundamentals in order to make it on this very difficult journey.

Learn from the master. Pete had the key to happiness and inner peace. He survived two World Wars, the Great Depression, and life's economic peaks and valleys. I am lucky enough to be the son of this great man, and I'm proud of it. In the pages that follow, you, the reader will be able to look at his Book of Knowledge and learn the life lessons that I was taught. My one regret is that it took me too long to learn what I was privileged enough to be generously taught every day from the smartest man I ever met, my dad.

Perhaps this quotation will sum up the reason this story needed to be told:

"There is not a man living, however poor

he may be, but has it in his power to

leave a heritage to those that follow him

the grandest thing on earth: Character."

Author unknown

Chapter 1

ITALIAN HARLEM 1910

Pete, my dad, was a no nonsense kid who grew up to be a no nonsense man. His life lessons started early. Near his tenement was the expansive East River. It was called Italian Harlem at the turn of the twentieth century, going from First Avenue and Pleasant Avenue, just six blocks long from 114th Street to 120th Street. The cobblestone streets were lined with tenements, families sitting on the fire escapes or on the stoops in the evenings to keep cool. The elevated transit ran through Harlem, as did the tracks of the trolleys.

The Italian immigrants were at the bottom of the economic scale; New York City alone in 1910 housing approximately 350,000 of the immigrants. It was hard for them to get work. They did not speak English and stayed together in their own little ghettos. The two biggest areas of concentration were Italian Harlem where Pete lived, and Little Italy at the southern end of the island at Mott and Mulberry Street, where his future wife would grow up.

Little Italy is now well known throughout our country for the famous Feast of San Gennaro.

They all came through Ellis Island; there were no quotas in those days. There was no work in Italy, and they were all looking for the American dream. Two million Italians came through Ellis Island between 1900 and 1920; only the Irish and Germans immigrated more.

The immigrants spoke different dialects, depending upon the part of Italy they came from. Few could read or write either English or Italian. Most of these immigrants were men; one in four planning on making their fortunes here; then going back to their own country to marry, build homes, and raise families.

These older areas of overcrowded tenements had poor sanitation; and sadly, tuberculosis ran rampant. Kids hung around outside, playing and sometimes getting into trouble. Pete's family went to their church of choice, Our Lady of Mount Carmel on 115th Street,. The Catholic service was conducted by an Italian priest in their native language. Most of the Italian immigrants living in this pocket of New York

City went to Mount Carmel. There were churches closer to Pete's house, but they were for the Irish and Germans; each group going to the place where familiar sounds could be heard and understood. The Italian immigrants emphasized family, church, and fraternal societies. Five had sprouted up in Pete's little corner of the world, and the Boy's Club had just opened to give the children a place to hang out.

There was little or no money, there was nothing to do. Kids went outside early in the day, entertaining themselves, and coming home for meals.

Pete's mom would yell out the window for her dependable son, "Pietro, vene qui," (Peter come here) needing him to help with something, or be her official translator to English. His parents had come from Naples, Italy. The tenements were too small to hang out in. Besides, you were not allowed to be underfoot, especially in the large families that were common at that time. You had to get out of the house while mom cooked and took care of the younger kids, not yet able to fend for themselves.

At age six, Pete had already realized he would not be able to play outside like the other kids. He had to plan on starting to work, to step up to the plate, knowing that he needed to help his mother and family financially. Yes, Pete was still a kid, but his father, Gabriel, was lazy, he didn't want to work and never did. In fact, Pete would begin his first job as a shoe shine boy a short time later.

But today Pete was enjoying the day, walking along with his friends on the pier by the East River, not far from his house. All of a sudden, one of the older kids, a hooligan, picked little Pete up and threw him into the river. Keep in mind when this happened, Pete was only six; furthermore, he did not know how to swim.

Let's stop here for a moment and think about if this had happened to one of our own children, especially at such a young age. What would they do? Could our children survive, or would they drown?

This is what little Pete did: He started flailing around to stay afloat. He saw that about twenty feet away was one of the pylons holding up the pier that he'd been thrown off. He had only two choices to make. One was to sink and drown. The other was to somehow make it to that pylon. The survival skills that Pete was born with kicked in. He used the stroke that is called the "dog paddle", and began to pump his arms and kick his feet vigorously. In what probably seemed to be a lifetime for him, Pete finally made it to that pylon and held on for dear life.

He yelled up to his friend: "Jots! Help me. Go find some rope and throw it down to me. Tie the rope around this thing I am holding on to."

Jots, Pete's best friend, knew better than to jump in after Pete, for he could not swim either. Thank goodness Jots was there to help.

12

Jots ran to his house which was only one block away and grabbed some clothes line rope, and hurried back to Pete. Jots knew that time was important. He tied the rope to one end of the pier and threw the other end to Pete, who was bravely holding on. Pete pulled on the rope, testing to see if it was safe and secure, and slowly started the climb, hand over hand, up the rope to the pier. He grabbed the pier and, breathing heavily, climbed up onto it.

While this was going on, all the other kids on the pier were laughing heartily, for they did not realize the seriousness or the possible consequences that could have come of their little prank. This experience that led to Pete's conquering the fear of water stayed with him for the rest of his life; for he loved to go to the ocean, swimming out farther than a little speck on the horizon, alone in his own space, just him and the sea.

You have just met Jots, Pete's best friend. Pete did not have much time for play. Once he started working, that was pretty much all he did. He also didn't have time for church. His mother knew that Pete had strong religious values, and she also knew he thought that bringing money home to feed the family took precedence over attending church. She accepted what was, and said special prayers, just for him.

Whenever there was time for a little enjoyment and fun, little Pete would still be a child; he and Jots would jump on the back of a trolley and head out. One of their favorite trips was going to the 125th Street correctional facility, to climb the walls up to a ledge, sit down legs dangling, and watch the prisoners in the yard. It must have made an indelible impression. Pete had no real trouble with the law, even down to never getting a speeding ticket in his entire life.

On one trip they were not very lucky. The twosome jumped the trolley, a simple childish prank common for all kids during that time. The conductor caught the two little hellions and threw them off the back of the caboose. Pete landed hard, right on his head in between the tracks, paved with gravel, leaving a large open gash with profuse bleeding. Pete, the ultimate survivor, did not want to miss the day of fun, as they were so rare. He just put his slosh cap down farther over his eyes to cover and tighten the wound, to help stop the bleeding. The two pals jumped on the next trolley and kept going, spending the day as planned.

When Pete came home, his mother saw that his little slosh cap was pulled almost completely over his right eye. She looked at it closer and saw that the cap was a dark red in color. She asked her son in Italian, "Cosa hai fatto?" (What have you done?) as she pulled the cap from his head. She saw that it was filled with blood coming from a deep gash above his right eye.

She grabbed a towel from the kitchen, wrapped it around his head and tied a knot. In the next minute she was pulling little Pete down the stairs by the hand. In her haste on this cool autumn evening, she forgot to grab her sweater causing her to feel a chill from the cold air, sending small shocks through her thin blouse. This enhanced her fear as she headed to the closest hospital in the area.

The doctor observed the mother arriving in a frantic state. He came to the aid of the young boy, removed the towel tied around his head, and saw the large gash, still dripping blood. He took Pete into a room where he began to treat the wound, which required twenty-seven stitches to his forehead. Pete never said a word or cried.

For little Pete, the scar that came as his wound healed became his badge of honor. Although faint, the scar remained until his death, a reminder of his young life, his friend Jots, and the day the conductor tossed the two of them off the caboose. Jots was the only person Pete ever called his best friend in his entire life.

This experience stayed with Pete and he used it to teach me the value of friendship. Someone I thought of as a friend had disappointed me after making a promise he didn't keep. I was nine years old at the time.

My dad said, "Come here, son, I want to show you something. Look at my hands," as he held them open in front of my face. He repeated, "Look at my hands, son." One by one, slowly and deliberately, he started to lower the fingers on his hands. First one hand closed and he lowered it down to his side, leaving one hand facing me. Then, the fingers of his second hand started to go down one by one. I stared at the two fingers left.

Dad asked, "How many fingers are left, son?"

I replied, "Two, Dad. Why?"

He continued to hold up the two fingers. "There are many people out there who may say that they're your friend, but are just acquaintances you may meet on this journey called life. The two fingers I am still holding up are the friends you may actually have in your life."

However, after lowering his final finger, leaving one finger in a direct line to my eyes and smiling that famous look of wisdom, Dad said, "If you end your life with one true friend, you are one lucky and contented man."

I heard that lesson from Dad many times over the years… I heard him, but I did not listen. That is two very different things. I did what so many of us do, I made friends quickly, talked too much – often about things that should have remained with me only. Many of these so-called friends were really just users, gossipmongers, jealous, ignorant, or malicious people who were nothing more than acquaintances. We don't always judge correctly in seeking friends. Now, I can honestly say, "I am one lucky and contented man because I have had two true friends in my life, I am a millionaire."

Pete always worked to support the family; it must have felt like forever, continually graduating to jobs that paid more, he was always hustling. The jobs were all hard manual labor, as he went from his shoe shining, to ice wagon and dirty laundry jobs.

Pete knew about the little restaurant on the corner, founded in 1896 by Charlie Rao. It was on 114th Street and Pleasant Avenue, three blocks from his house. He passed it every day and noticed that some of the older Italian men were dressed eloquently, flashing around a great deal of money, while hanging out at this small place.

Pete, never shy when it came to making a buck, just showed up at the back door one day. Thinking quickly, he told Charlie, "I can keep this place cleaner than any other kid in the neighborhood." Then without missing a beat, Pete sprang into action, knowing instinctively that the window of opportunity was opening a sliver, and it could shut just as quickly. He picked up a broom and started sweeping.

Charlie watched this self-assured young kid with an infectious smile; guessed he was around twelve or thirteen. Pete did not slow down. He was in high gear and before Charlie knew what was happening, Pete had the place shining. He had walked briskly past all the men, minded his business, but with an upbeat way about him.

Pete came back day after day, washed dishes, swept the front, washed the windows, and always smiled. The men liked him, and a few started giving him small tips. This felt great, more money to bring home to mom. He stayed there for a few years, doing well for himself.

Pete had never totally given up his shoe shine business, even as he climbed up the money chain. Frankie, his younger brother, had once brought the box down to Pete's corner to play with, when Pete moved on to harder labor. Pete caught Frankie, who was seven years younger than himself, when he came home from working on the ice wagon; Pete grabbed the box from him. It was one of the few times he ever yelled at his brother.

"That box is not a toy. It is how I earn a living for the family. Don't ever touch it again!"

After that, the box stayed in its place at home – until Pete saw an opportunity.

One day he brought his shoe shine kit to Rao's.

Charlie said, "Okay kid, if you mind your own business and my customers want a shine, you can go for it." Charlie knew that the more comfortable the men felt, the more they would drink, eat, and talk with their friends, spending time and money in his establishment.

The Italians were making their mark in this little restaurant, establishing political connections, and finding ways to use their influence. Pete just worked; he listened, minded his own business, and worked some more.

Today, Rao's still stands on the corner of 114th Street and Pleasant Avenue, rebuilt after it burned down accidentally after 1970, a testimony to what connections can do. There are only ten tables, with only one seating every night. The good, the bad, the ugly, the people in politics, sports, entertainment, whoever pulls the right strings go there to see and be seen. All fresh ingredients are brought in daily, most flown in from Italy. All dishes are made to taste, whatever the special diner desires. It is an epicurean delight… if you are one of the powerful men and women in New York City lucky enough to get in. It is a closed society; to this day you probably will not get a reservation. You must be a "star" in the political world, the sports or entertainment world, or have the right connection. You know what I'm talking about, don't you? The strings are still controlled and pulled by the Rao family, in business for 115 years and going. That's quite an accolade.

Pete realized that he could not juggle school and work, and so his formal education ended. He knew he couldn't be everywhere; the family needed money more than he needed to go to school, so the little bit of childhood remaining ended.

As he grew stronger, it was time to bring home more money. Pete started working construction, anything that came up. He dug ditches, carried up to one hundred bricks at a time pushing a wheelbarrow on construction sites. He worked the dirty part of laying a roof, all the messiest jobs, knowing he could get more money for that kind of work. He always told the employer that he could do the job. He worked anywhere he could make a buck. He never disappointed. His mind thought of only this: work, provide, and survive.

Peter always knew that his father, Gabriel, was not happy in New York City. He did not like the crowds, the hustle and bustle, the kids on the street, and the new mob element that was invading the neighborhood. He did not talk much about it, but the time he was arrested in the park had a big effect on him.

Gabriel had gone for a walk in Central Park one day, its most northern part at 110th Street; he'd carried his rifle with him. He sat on a bench and proceeded to shoot at pigeons that would fly by. He was planning to bring the birds home for dinner. Instead, he was arrested by New York's finest. He had shot pigeons and quails as a young boy in the countryside near Naples, Italy and did not see why he couldn't do the same in New York City. As far as Gabriel was concerned, he did nothing wrong.

Pete's mother had to go to the local precinct and get him released, promising up and down that he would never do that again.

That may sound like it was easy, but not so. My grandmother had to bring her son, Pete, my father, with her to translate, as she did not speak English. The police who were mostly Irish, loved to make it difficult for the Italians. After all, the Irish came to this country and found good jobs in construction, on the police force, as firemen, all because they already spoke the language, albeit with a heavy accent. They considered the Italians to be beneath them, bringing bad blood throughout that whole generation – that is, until the next generation of English speaking Italians changed that. But it took a long time, and the Irish were always one or two steps ahead of the Italians on the food chain, making more money and letting their feud fuel over for a long time. And this was especially evident in NYC.

Gabriel was a mean, narcissistic, selfish man, who did not like being told what to do. That became clear after the arrest. His wife and his children had always feared him; due to his vicious temper, and his demeaning language. The beatings for all were also part of life in the family. All his children knew to never speak to or about their father in a derogatory way. The anger intensified after the arrest as did the violence.

Pete was always respectful to his father out of his admiration and love for his mother. There were times when his father was abusive, especially to his mother. Pete had to override his resentment and restrain himself. He knew he could hurt his father if he wanted to, but never would. It would go against what his mother expected of him.

Pete always wanted to be a New York City fireman. As a young boy, the sounds of the sirens sent young Pete's heart racing. He'd drop everything and run after the horse drawn bright red fire wagons, watching in fascination the strong men aboard, and their uniforms enhancing their brawny look. These were NY's firemen charging ahead, saving lives, and putting out those fierce fiery waves of destruction that were reaching toward the sky, lighting it up for all to see. Pete began to plan.

When Pete turned twenty he took the exam, and passed it. He knew the wages he'd earn would help his family considerably, and looked forward to his future working as a NYC fireman. Pete waited anxiously for an opening. He knew it might take time but it would be worth the wait. The years passed and he was getting closer to his goal.

Gabriel Cicale (Father) with pipe and friend, early 1900s

Pete's confirmation at 12 years old, with family friend

Chapter 2

GABRIEL TAKES A TRIP

Pete's father had another idea of what the family was going to do and planned accordingly. Gabriel was always going somewhere on a trip or disappearing for hours on end. He frequented the private Italian social clubs, also enjoying the saloons around New York. Gabriel was often resting from not working and no one dared say a word. It was a given in the family that the father did what he wanted to, without question and without reprisal.

Pete knew that whatever his father said or appeared to state always had repercussions or surprises attached; as Gabriel announced his summer vacation: "I'm going north by myself, to the Hudson Valley area of New York." Instincts and street smarts made Pete leery, and a feeling of dread arose inside him.

Gabriel, this selfish lazy man, not to mention a philanderer, bought a new summer suit costing fifteen dollars, which was a lot of money back then. But money was never a problem when it came to treating himself, and Gabriel was preparing to take his trip come hell or high water.

He descended down the front steps of their tenement, all dapper and strutting, satchel in hand, smiling slyly as he headed out for his trip up north, destination New Paltz, New York, a place rapidly becoming a popular vacation spot.

As a kid, I often wondered how Grandpa, who never worked a day in his life, always managed to have so much money. It only came to light after my father, Pete, died. I finally found out how my grandfather allegedly had the money to make thirteen trips back and forth to Italy before the turn of the twentieth century. Family folklore tells it this way: It seems that Gabriel was left an orphan in Naples as a young child, the result of an accident that had killed his parents. He had no close relatives to raise him. A member of the well known Delonghi family adopted Gabriel. The story passed down is that the adopted father was a powerful man in Naples.

This is the same family name that we see in stores today on the labels of small appliances and coffeemakers. The family business was started in Italy and proved successful around the world. In fact,

I own a Delonghi coffeemaker. Is this story true? I do not know.

Gabriel kept his last name, Cicale, but the family believes he enjoyed the perks and money he reaped from the Delonghi relationship. Perhaps that explains the reason for his feeling of entitlement; his not working for a living. No one really knows how much money he had, Gabriel was a secretive man and his money was always well hidden from the rest of his family.

By the way, I was named after this man, my grandfather, Gabriel; a man who was detested by all the family. But any of his grandchildren who were named after him, the parents received five hundred dollars, an enormous amount of money at that time. There are six or seven Gabriel's in the family. Was it out of respect or solely for the money? I really don't know. All the same, I love my name, just not the source.

Back to my story, Gabriel returned to NYC and the usually arrogant, uncommunicative man took his wife aside. He told her about his new plan. Then this misanthrope, who never cared for anyone, who never thought of anyone but himself, called all of his family together to tell them what was going to be taking place.

The family conversation – if you can call one person speaking and everyone else sitting around as captive listeners – began. Gabriel only did what he wanted, and if the domino effect that might follow was to occur afterwards, that was something he thought nothing about. He briefly described his journey, ending with a giant bombshell: the family was moving to almost four hundred acres he had purchased in upstate New York, in a small hamlet called Milton to become farmers. He did not put it up for debate. He told the family that they were leaving soon.

Gabriel boasted about his trip up the Hudson River on the newest luxury steamboat called the Washington Irving. He talked about the beautiful full foliage of summer he saw along the way.

The property that they were moving to came with a large white two story house, along with other buildings on the property. That was all the information they were going to receive. In Gabriel's inimitable way, he always played it close to the vest.

Gabriel then arrogantly stated that when they went up the river to their new home, he could use his rifle and shoot all the birds he wanted to, without being arrested. It was an area that reminded him of his youth, reminiscent of the countryside outside of Naples, where he grew up. He ended his one way conversation by saying that he was headed back to the valley in two weeks with the remainder of the money for his land. It would be a short trip and he was taking Pete with him, leaving the rest of the family behind this one time.

Pete knew the reason he was accompanying his father. He was going to be the one who would work and support everyone wherever they went. It was a trip based on necessity, not favoritism. He'd be the one doing the farming.

Dad sat there quiet and stunned. What about his dream of becoming a fireman? His mother turned to him, the only woman in the world he would do anything for, put her hand gently on his, and quietly in her heavy Italian dialect implored, "Pietro, per favore, vai con tuo padre. Quando la famiglia sitrasferisce in campagna a devi venire con me." (Peter, please go with your father. When the family moves to the country, you must come with me.)

Pete did not wallow in misery over the fact that he could not be a fireman. Instead, he used common sense, as he always had before. Pete knew that two brothers, Michael, who was now twenty-six, Tony who was twenty, and one sister, Vincenza, who was twenty-four, would not be going with them. They were all staying in New York with their future spouses. The brothers had never helped him support the family anyway. And Pete's four remaining sisters and his younger brother, Frank, would all be going up north to live on the property Gabriel had purchased. The family all presumed that Pete would be the one to tend the farm, and that was just the way it was going to be.

Pete knew that he would be their meal ticket; as usual it would be his responsibility to provide for them. Pete worried about the family, especially his mother. He did not have much time to dwell on what was about to happen. He was uncomfortable thinking about it. He had never spent time alone with his father. It turned out to be the only time that he and his father's life would intertwine whether for good or bad.

When I asked Dad why he didn't refuse to go and do as he wished, he told me: "My responsibility to the family was always my first priority. I needed to help Mother, and my father was not going to do that." I didn't understand how he could give up his dream. He just looked at me serenely and said another one of his *Peteisms*, "Son, never expect and you'll never be disappointed."

And so it went that Dad left New York City for the Hudson Valley, eighty miles upstate, to become a farmer, which he knew absolutely nothing about. But Pete was a quick study; his survival instincts would have to take over once again.

Chapter 3

AN UNUSUAL JOURNEY
FOR PETE

The time went quickly; after the big announcement that the family was moving, the apartment was all abuzz. Everyone had to make decisions. The future would be different for all of them.

A few days passed without anyone hearing more about the move. Gabriel, who did things solely for his own needs, awoke in time for lunch. Pete was at the table. He had come in for something to eat, in between jobs. Gabriel informed Pete that they were going shopping downtown that same afternoon.

Pete already had plans. He was expecting to help a nearby family, who was moving away from the neighborhood. It was going to be a fast buck for Pete, but now he had a dilemma on his hands.

Pete, the dutiful son, had to obey his father. Yet, he also knew he had an obligation to do the job. Once Pete committed himself to do something, he did it. He glanced at this younger brother, Frankie, only fifteen years old, and knew the he had found the solution; he would send Frankie in his place.

Pete accompanied his father to the downtown haberdasher. He had never been in a store such as this, filled with all the finery of the day.

Mr. Garrola greeted his father with strong familiarity. "Buona giornata mio caro amico." (Good day, my dear friend.)

Pete was instructed to stand on a small platform; the two older men walked the store, and came back with some things for him to try on. Pete's entire wardrobe was made up of hand-me-downs. But, Gabriel was obviously outfitting him for the trip north to the Hudson Valley. They did not talk, Pete did as was directed, and he left the store carrying: a new serge grey suit with a long belted jacket and matching knickerbockers pants, two white dress shirts, spats, a satin tie, new oxford shoes, and socks.

When Pete arrived home that day he immediately went to the neighbor's to make sure that his brother had done the work that Pete had promised to take care of. He found out the job had gone smoothly.

Pete was proud of Frankie, also happy that he had personally taken care of the situation; for Pete it was a win-win situation.

Pete taught us, his children, something he applied that day, a code he lived by all his life. It was a very often repeated *Peteism* in our home. Dad said, "Your word is your bond. It is the only thing you have in life. Do not ever lose it."

The day for the trip north came soon thereafter. Gabriel, a real Beau Brummell, dressed in one of his summer suits, and Pete dressed in his new clothing, headed out. Directly in front of the house a horse and buggy awaited them. The entire trip was first class, something Pete would never want, or care about, for the rest of his life.

They came to the pier and boarded the Washington Irving, the same large elegant day liner that his father had taken on his first journey. There were a few thousand people on the steamboat as it set up the Hudson River; the very same river that Hendrick Hudson had discovered and explored in 1609 with his sailboat the Half Moon.

Although Pete was a novice at traveling by water, he was unafraid. He knew that if something happened onboard, he would be able to swim. He had learned that at six years old in the East River, thanks to his fearlessness and the help of his friend, Jots.

The new life experience started with something as simple as boarding the steam liner. There were some very fancy gentlemen and ladies coming aboard, many having their luggage carried by servants or porters, black men dressed in black outfits, white shirts and shiny high button shoes. The passengers were very jolly, smiling happily.

Gabriel took on a whole new persona, strutting with the best of them, obviously used to this kind of luxury; a note filed and imbedded in his son's brain for the rest of his life. Pete wondered why they had been living so humbly, when this man, his father, was now flashing wads of cash around.

The Washington Irving started north, moving slowly. Pete stood on deck transfixed by what he saw. The scenery was spectacular, wide open space laid before him.

He inhaled the purified air. It was a clear summer day; the aroma was foreign to Pete's nose. It was fresh and clean, devoid of all the pollutants of NYC. The trees were full with the vibrant greens of summer; a shower of so many different shades of that beautiful color filled the shores on both sides of the river.

The trip took the better part of the day and Pete was forced to relax. There was nowhere to go, no timeframe to do something in, Pete could only people watch from the deck. The homes along the Hudson sat high and majestic, as if built into the mountains. Pete had never seen a mountain before, except in school books, and that was a long time ago.

Pete chuckled to himself, thinking of his neighborhood, the street in East Harlem. All of the families on his block, perhaps 500 people, maybe more, could have filled the empty space between each home, and there would still have been room left over for grass.

The boat kept moving north bringing with it more spectacular views. Bigger mountains, larger expanses, it appeared to Pete that he could see as far away as forever.

When the boat began to slow down, Pete glanced up at the largest bridge he had ever seen. One of the deck hands told him, "You're looking at the old railroad bridge, completed in 1889, that connects Poughkeepsie and Highland."

The railroad was already thriving, bringing fifty freight trains a day through the area. The trains carried the products of the region, the produce and other crops from the west side of the Hudson to the east at Poughkeepsie, for distribution to all the surrounding states.

Pete also saw the construction going on nearby for the Poughkeepsie Bridge, which would later be renamed the Mid Hudson Bridge. He could see a large crew of men working at that site. The new bridge would also connect the two sides of the Hudson, from Highland to Poughkeepsie. It was the 1920s and would open soon, in 1930, allowing horses and buggies, as well as cars for the relatively affluent, to cross the river. It would speed the journey for the commonality, who wanted to go across for pleasure or business purposes.

The Washington Irving pulled into Poughkeepsie, at Lattimer's Landing and everyone disembarked. Pete stayed near his father. Many people were waiting at the landing to get on. The boat would turn around at this point and head back down the river completing its day trip.

Gabriel led the way as they joined a group of people heading to a small ferry. It would take them across the Hudson to the west side of the river at Highland. Father and son boarded for the short trip across the water. Upon arrival on the west shore, Gabriel told Pete that their new home was nearby, but they wouldn't see it until the next day.

His father wanted to complete the trip to their final destination by heading to New Paltz six miles farther west. They took a trolley to the place where Gabriel had stayed on his previous trip. He pointed out the land, the awe inspiring Shawangunk Mountains, an Indian name that sounds strange in English, but even worse in the Italian that his father spoke.

They viewed some of the spacious farms and a wide variety of crops growing on the cleared parcels of land. There was also a great deal of barren land, some made ready for farming. Pete absorbed all he saw, his father pointing things out with minimal dialogue. They exited the trolley at New Paltz, a town where some of the original white settlers, the Huguenots, all English speaking, had settled in the early 1600s.

His father had repeated his original trip to show Pete why he had selected this area to buy land. He also wanted to convince himself, one last time, that he had made the right choice, by seeing it again with clear eyes, before completing his last financial transaction for the land.

Gabriel was not a worker, but he was a shrewd man. He liked what he had seen on his vacation to the area. His trip had been enlightening; he had found new acquaintances, all from the old country, all speaking Italian as their primary and usually only language. Apparently there were others like himself who felt it was time to move farther away from the problems of a large city.

They were staying at the same boarding house where Gabriel had previously enjoyed himself. That point was emphasized when the owner, Rosie, a flirty buxom blonde, greeted Gabriel intimately upon their arrival.

Pete looked on awkwardly at the familiarity between the two, but said nothing. He knew his father well, and was not surprised by his behavior. Gabriel had his own life in NYC, enjoying his freedom with other women, hanging out at the saloons, the Italian social clubs, and the speakeasies that were sprouting up in the city. The only thing that would change in Gabriel's life when the family moved was the area where he'd continue to live his decadent lifestyle.

In 1920, Prohibition had taken root. NYC was ripe for any way to make a fast buck. A new breed of men called "bootleggers" were unafraid to get involved in illegal activities, had little fear of reprisals, and were having a field day. These men were greedy, slimy entrepreneurs, taking advantage of the times. They were providing the illegal alcohol for the workers; stills were making white alcohol, which was to imitate the real stuff for all the classes as well.

The most daring of these new entrepreneurs were bringing in the real alcohol, coming over from Europe and entering the hot commodity through Canada, making many men very wealthy. Joseph Kennedy, father of our late President, John Fitzgerald Kennedy, was one of them.

Pete also thought that this might be one of the reasons why his father was heading up to this area. The mafia, or Cosa Nostra, this unsavory cadre formed in Sicily in the middle of the nineteenth century, was starting to vie for dibs on all the illegal activity that was creeping into New York City, forever changing the infrastructure there. Pete knew that his father was friends with a lot of the guys in the mob, maybe too friendly, and he wondered if Gabriel was really thinking about his family when he bought the land in the Hudson Valley. Yes, he was getting his children out of the element, but was it really for the children or more for himself?

Pete found it hard to juggle all these new thoughts in his head, for he firmly believed that Gabriel was the most narcissistic person ever, who would normally not even think about his family. Pete's only concern was that he had to protect his mother and siblings, at all costs. To hell with his father, as long as he kept his hands to himself; he had become more violent in recent years, not only verbally but physically.

Even more confusing to Pete was that the charmer he traveled with now was not the father he knew in the city. Gabriel was warm and funny, engaging in small talk with the other summer boarders, most of them visiting the area for the same reason as his father, to purchase land.

Coincidentally, also staying at the boarding house was another Italian immigrant who was making his return visit there. That man was my mother's father, Dominick Porpiglia. They both had selected the same place to settle, the small hamlet of Milton.

Along with the two small adjoining towns of Marlboro and Highland, the whole area encompassed five miles, a little pocket in New York for Italians migrating north. The area had 800 inhabitants at the beginning of the 1920s.

The middle class that was starting to populate this area called the Hudson Valley was a steady moral thinking and working class. The migration north encompassed what are now Dutchess, Orange, Rockland, Ulster, and Westchester counties.

Although the area itself dates back at least 8,000 years, the Indians had little or no impact on the land and the terrain; never abusing their natural habitat. Some of the tribes who inhabited that territory were the Iroquois, Lenape, and the Mohawk.

It was only when the white settlers arrived, during and after the Industrial Revolution, in the mid nineteenth century that change started to happen. In 1845 in the Hudson River environs, only 75 years earlier, the first market grape vineyard had been planted by William Cornell. There were even Catholic churches going up in the valley; the earliest, Saint Joseph's Roman Catholic Church, was erected in New Paltz in 1894. The first fire company was established there a few years earlier in 1889.

A great deal was happening and many changes were occurring. Of course, the biggest challenge for Pete would be to become a farmer. He was puzzled by all this new stimulation, terrified and excited at the same time.

Gabriel and Pete settled in. Gabriel had generously paid for two rooms but Pete believed the sole reason was so his father could have privacy to do whatever he wanted. Pete noted that his room was at the very opposite end of the long hall from his father's.

Gabriel instructed his son, "Vai in camera tua disimballare e ripulire," (Go to your room, unpack and clean up.)

Pete mumbled, "Si, Padre," (Yes, father) and hurried off.

Pete was excited to see the room he would sleep in for a few nights. It would be the first time he had his own room, the privacy something he had never even dreamed of. He was used to sharing a room with his three brothers.

While Pete was gone, Gabriel arranged for a horse and buggy to take them to dinner.

Pete returned within fifteen minutes to find his father socializing. He heard a hearty laugh coming from his father. He stood quietly in the vestibule, not really knowing if he should join the conversation.

Gabriel saw Pete, excused himself from the other boarders, and motioned for Pete to follow him.

When they went outside the carriage was already waiting to take the twosome to the Mohonk Mountain Lodge, a magnificent fieldstone and log hotel known far and wide for opulence and its celebrity guests, some of the most influential people of the day.

They arrived at the front entrance and a man in uniform helped the twosome disembark from the carriage. Pete thought he saw his father discreetly give the man money, but couldn't be sure. They walked up the stairs entering the lobby which led to an expansive reception area. Couches were situated all around; men and women, dressed to the nines, were engrossed in conversation. His father walked to the dining room without saying a word. He obviously had been there before. Pete knew that he was to see and be seen, but not heard, so he followed behind Gabriel at an appropriate distance.

The food was like nothing he had ever tasted before; it was not his mother's delicious Italian cooking, or the fancy Italian meals served at Rao's. This was what it was like to eat American continental cuisine, whatever that was. His father ordered for him. The tastes Pete experienced were foreign to his palate, but quite filling. Pete savored the moment, for he knew this was not going to be the norm in his life, nor did he want it to be. He preferred his mother's cooking. Pete was a simple young man and he enjoyed the comfort of being in his own skin, without pretense. He did not care for this showiness.

But, for now, he would just indulge himself. Besides, what else could he do?

The stately Mohonk Mountain Lodge, overlooking the Hudson River still thrives today, a wonderful vacation place that brings one back to the elegance and spectacular building techniques utilized when it was first erected so long ago.

The following morning Pete awoke early. The other boarders were all asleep. He dressed quickly and headed outside, taking in the sights and smells of the countryside around him. How strange it felt. He heard birds singing, He witnessed the area come to life, as people came into town.

Many came by wagon to stock up at the large general store nearby. Pete entered the store. The proprietor knew everybody by name. He had a big book where he wrote down all the things the people were buying, and everyone spoke in perfect English. That was not the case at the boarding house, where he heard Italian as the primary language. No wonder his father liked it there.

Pete checked out a few of the other stores in the busy town then headed back to Rosie's place and waited for his father to come down for breakfast. Gabriel finally appeared in the dining room two hours later. They sat down to plates piled high with bacon, eggs, pancakes, and homemade biscuits; all served by Rosie herself, the overly friendly owner.

She again doted on Gabriel; his father openly flirting back at her.

Pete felt uncomfortable. His eyes glanced elsewhere to other patrons in the room. He knew that Gabriel did not need permission for his boorish behavior. He did whatever he wanted to, and this morning he was intent on charming Rosie.

His father finally remembered him, and succinctly told Pete the agenda for the day: "Stiamo andando a visitare la citta poi viaggiare alla nuova casa." (We're going to tour the town, then travel to the new home.)

Their first stop was at the bank, "Aspetta qui," (Wait here) his father pointed to a chair inside the main room.

Gabriel then went into a private office to sign some papers. Pete was along on this trip for one reason – to learn about the area, not to be privy to anything that had to do with his father's money, and/or the land purchase. They exited the bank and his father actually smiled. Pete guessed that he was happy with his decision.

They walked around New Paltz, his father showing him the vibrant town. Pete did not comment. He was glad he had already done this on his own, earlier that morning; this second trip around the town helped reinforce what was now becoming familiar to him.

They went back on the trolley into Highland, and took a horse and buggy to travel through the outlying area. Gabriel showed Pete all the working farms. He pointed out several other parcels of land for sale. They also went past the small stores that would service tiny Milton. He told him that the locals would have to travel the short distance to New Paltz for a larger selection of goods.

They reached their destination; the large parcel of property that would soon be home. The homestead that Gabriel had purchased was not far from the Hudson River, the sloops and steamboats were part of the beautiful backdrop.

Gabriel walked up the road to the main house with an intense feeling of pride, for he had achieved the American dream: land ownership and the acquiring of land as a symbol of wealth, everything that he had come to this country for. They stopped at the large white two story main house on the property, built before the turn of the twentieth century, and walked to the front entrance. A large wide porch the width of the house greeted them. The house itself looked majestic.

The house had no occupants. It was an estate sale. They did not have a key yet to go inside, and walked the grounds instead. Behind the main house sat what was called a summer kitchen, to be used for cooking and entertaining.

A family summer kitchen was not uncommon for Italian immigrants. It was a place to cook, without bringing the heat of the summer into the main house. It was a separate or second kitchen that the immigrant Italians loved so much. The summer kitchen on the property had few windows, but was primarily made of screening, perfect for warm weather.

Later, for the Cicale family, it would become an area for great times, for cooking and eating at a big family table. But the real enjoyment would be the harmony, the singing, and laughing that would engulf the whole family; those who would be living in the valley and the family members who would come to visit, those who had stayed behind in NYC. They would all join in on glorious hot Sunday afternoons, where five or six courses of food would be served.

The land also came with barns which could house livestock such as cows, sheep, goats, horses, pigs, and chickens. There were additional barns and sheds on the land that could be used for housing some of the equipment, tools, and supplies, to take care of everything that a working farm entailed. His father showed him another building that would be used for a packing house to sort fruits and vegetables that would be grown on the farm. That was all they did that day, and Pete went back to the boarding house absorbed in thought.

Pete compared his present and future homes; the differences were dramatic. Back in East Harlem, their apartment housed eleven members of the family. In addition, the smells of the many inhabitants of his building living so close together was the only thing he could really relate to. Their apartment was so small. It had a wood burning stove with a brick bathtub in the center of the kitchen. When the brick tub was not used for bathing, they would put wooden planks over it; thus becoming the kitchen table. There were three other families on their floor, all sharing two common bathrooms. Their family was one of the smaller ones on his floor. One of their neighbors had eighteen people living in the same size apartment as them. The other two also had larger families than his.

He knew that they paid $10.00 a month rent; he had always been privy to that information. After all, he was the breadwinner, never really having had a childhood. He imagined what it would be like to live on all this land and how the family would adapt; but mostly he worried about the burden of making the land work.

The next few days helped Pete overcome some of his doubts. Father and son spent the next day together. They took the trolley back to the area where their new home was, but did not stop at the house this time. Instead, they went to a few of the local farms to look around. They were met warmly, for all the neighbors were immigrants like themselves who readily spoke Italian with Gabriel, and were helpful in answering their many questions.

Chapter 4

A CRASH COURSE

The following two days, Gabriel gave Pete some money and sent him off by himself to explore the region. Pete was relieved, for he was always on guard around his father.

By nature, Pete was a shy man, but he was smart enough to know that he now had to get down to business if he was going to start farming. It would have to be a crash course.

First thing, Pete went to New Paltz General Store to pick up a large notebook to write down all he was about to learn. He then jumped on the trolley and headed back to Milton.

He then went back to the same farms he'd visited the day before. His first stop was the nearby

Guardino farm. Pete asked in Italian and English, a broken dialect, "Do you have some time to show me around?"

"Certamente," (certainly) and very slowly in English, Gino Guardino said, "I will help you with what I can."

Pete was relieved for he could speak in English about important information he needed to gather. "May I call you Gino? My name is Pete."

Yes," Gino said, "What do you know about farming?"

"I don't know a thing. I grew up in New York City. Have you always been a farmer?"

"Yes, my family had a farm in Italy. It is the only thing I know," said Gino.

Pete was prepared to learn. He said, "Let's walk around and I will write down what I need to know. Is that okay?"

And so the two men walked the land. Pete had questions about almost everything; he spoke freely. He asked a few pertinent questions, but mostly Pete listened as Gino explained the art of being a good farmer. Gino answered in full all of Pete's questions.

Pete knew he had someone who would help him. "Grazie, Gino, (Thank you, Gino), you are so kind. I will see you soon."

Pete did not stop with just one farm. He walked the dirt roads, looking everywhere. He wrote and drew pictures of everything he saw. Pete came to another farm they'd visited the day before. This time it was even easier. Signore Locamante was working alongside his son, Giuseppe.

Pete approached, remembering that they had spoken only Italian the previous day. And said to the elder man, "Buona giornata, prego posso inserici?" (Good day, may I please enter?)

The son answered in perfect English, much to Pete's relief. "Hi, I'm Joe Jr., and you have already met my father, Joseph. He told me that you and your father were here yesterday. How can I help you?"

Pete smiled and said, "Farming will be a new experience for my family. I have just been to the Guardino family farm and Gino was very helpful. I wonder if you would be so kind as to do the same... take me for a walk around your farm?"

Joe said, "I'll be happy to. I have some chores to do in the apple orchard and you can come with me."

Pete was thrilled for Joe was around his age, and they developed an instant rapport. They walked the orchard and Joe told him everything he knew about planting the crop. He explained how to get started; what Pete would need to buy, the animals he would need, the seedlings that would grow on the land in this part of the state, how to take care of a crop, fertilizing, how to pick and what to plant in each season.

Joe took him into the packing house as a special treat. It would soon be harvest time and they were preparing for the crop. Pete wrote and wrote, asked a lot of questions, and felt more and more in control, for he now had his starting point.

Pete understood how much Joe was helping him. He was smart enough to absorb all that was told. It was a life lesson that came out of his farming lessons and a *Peteism* he used throughout his life: "To learn you have to be a listener. You can't talk and listen at the same time."

When he returned to the boarding house, he did not talk much. He was very tired with all the questions and answers whirling through his head. He did not want to go to any fancy dinners, but to his surprise he was not even asked. Now, that was the father he knew.

Gabriel simply stated, "Io vado per la sera, e non c'e cibo la sciato per voi da mangiare." (I'm going out for the evening, and there is food left for you to eat.)

Pete was thrilled. He didn't show it. He simply said, "Andro via domani mattina presto." (I'll be going off early tomorrow morning.) He was assured that there would be a small meal left for him, as his father would be sleeping.

The next morning, Pete again headed to Milton. He visited one more farmer, Anthony Pancilli,, asking more questions. The farmer's wife, Antoinette, invited him for lunch. He now could see the inside of a home in the valley, and noticed all the things they would need to make their home comfortable and livable.

He had been told by his father that the estate had nothing indoors except the walls.. He remembered as much as possible and would write everything down when he left the Pancilli's.

How kind all these people were, how polite, and he enjoyed the macaroni that he knew and loved so well. The family spoke Italian. They laughed a lot, and told him that he would be happy here. He felt good. This was familiar to him, the meal, and the dialogue, even the laughing, which occurred freely.

Pete's family laughed too, especially when his father was not around. They suggested he go into town and look at the stores. They also confirmed that the big supplies were purchased in New Paltz, and he knew that he would stop there at the big general store before nightfall.

Pete went into Milton General Store and met the man working in the small local store. It was not the owner who was away. The owner's wife was having her fifth child. The worker, Louie, was so friendly and excited that Pete almost thought he was the one having a child.

Pete noticed the limitations of the store. He inquired about delivery times, for he now felt like he could ask intelligent questions. He wrote down prices for things he knew he would need. He felt he'd like to give the small town store as much business as he could, if the price was right. He would go back to New Paltz General Store and compare. He liked Louie, but prices and value would determine where he would make his purchases.

Pete always lived that way. "Anyone can pay retail," he'd say, "Get what you pay for. The smart man will shop and buy wholesale. That extra money you save goes in your pocket. If it is going to go into someone's pocket, it might as well be yours."

When I first heard this *Peteism*, it amazed me that he used it referring to money that would be coming from his father. But, no matter what he felt about the man, money from his father was family money.

In New Paltz, he could now speak with knowledge of his present situation. The conversations at the nearby farms and his first stop at the Milton General Store had given him the courage to take on the daunting task that lay before him. The family was going to live off the land; he had to plan on producing lucrative crops that were relevant. He knew it would take hard work to make the farm produce. Pete was never afraid of that. He knew he would have to cultivate the land. No matter. Pete was used to manual labor. Didn't he carry ice, wet laundry, do construction in NYC? Besides, there was no choice. The family had to survive and Pete, the ultimate survivor, had to make it happen.

He had quickly learned that the Hudson Valley's primary crops were apples and grapes, but the maturing process for them would take several years. The valley also grew peaches, strawberries, cherries, raspberries, and currants; almost any kind of fruit would grow on that dark rich soil. He could grow other fruits and vegetables that would have a shorter maturation process. He would plan for fast growing summer crops, a way to make a fast return on their invested monies. Pete was told that the summer crops could be picked every six weeks, allowing him more than one crop of each per season.

The land was perfect for agriculture. There was great grazing land for the animals that would join the family. No one owned lawn mowers, the sheep were used to graze the land – they were probably the first known self-powering mowers.

He priced out the things on his list, compared prices to the store in Milton, and knew precisely what he would need to get started, all the necessities for family life on the farm.

The following day the two men headed back to NYC. Pete took the opportunity to tell his father exactly what they'd need to get the farm up and working. He outlined his plan, the purchases of livestock, the seeds for crops, the tools that would have to be purchased, and the transportation they would need to subsequently take their intended crop to market.

Pete's limited formal education did not affect his ability to visualize in an orderly way. He had always planned his working time to maximize his efforts. He had his notebook in perfect order. His comparative prices were underlined, everything that he would need detailed, even furnishings for the home that he had written down after his visit to the Pancillis. It was an animated conversation; his father let him speak and agreed to all the things his son said, assuring him that he would acquire everything on Pete's list. His father took the notebook from him, the conversation was over.

If Gabriel was proud of his son and all that he had learned, he did not express it. And Pete did not expect it. Both men knew that Pete was the doer, and Gabriel would be the nonparticipating recipient of life on the farm. It was the only civil conversation they would have in Pete's lifetime.

Gabriel knew that Pete would somehow do the right thing. He really didn't care how it was done, as long as it got done. After all, he was bringing the family up north for a better life, and he was planning on resting peacefully. Gabriel saw himself as the gentleman farmer who would be sitting under some old shade tree, drinking a gallon of wine and eating a raw onion, which he would heartily do on a daily basis. Meanwhile, Pete, the mule, would do all the work.

Chapter 5

THE MOVE

The trip back to New York City had gone quickly. Pete had his father as a captive audience. Based on all their earlier interactions, Pete knew that he had to impress on his father the urgency of getting things prepared for life on the farm. He felt that he'd accomplished that. Gabriel rarely spoke to any family members; he had talked at them, a huge difference. The window of opportunity had opened for this very short period of time. Pete, hopefully, had gotten his message across.

His lesson to us, his children, following that meeting was this: "Don't talk just to hear yourself. When you have something important to contribute, make sure you get your point across."

His *Peteism* must have worked. By the time they arrived in NYC, Gabriel informed his son that he would be heading out again the following week to order and receive supplies at the new homestead.

Pete walked up the stairs of the sad looking tenement that was still their home. He had a lighter step to his walk. He started to visualize life on the farm, and for the first time, Pete was optimistic about his chances to pull it off. Now it was his job to alleviate the anxiety for the rest of his family.

Pete was gentle. He knew how to speak with all of his siblings, as well as to his mother. This was to be a monumental change in their lives and he decided to speak with each individually. Their entire world was going to be in an upheaval, he had to put out the fires of fear. It would be the only fires he would ever put out; his childhood dream of being a NYC fireman would never come to be.

But, Pete approached the future as he had everything else in his life. Survival was tantamount in his mind. He convinced everyone that they were headed for a great adventure. Did he really believe that? It did not matter; he could not waste precious time thinking about that. The land purchase was a fait accompli and he could not change their destiny.

He had little time left to say his good-byes. He managed to see Jots one last time. They promised to stay in touch. There were no telephones readily available to them, they didn't write letters, and

Pete never went back to the old neighborhood. Jots eventually moved away too. Although they lost contact and did not see each other for almost sixty years, Pete often talked about Jots in the present, as though they had been together just yesterday. And why not, wasn't Jots his best friend?

It was also quite difficult for the siblings staying behind. Good-byes were painful and the little that the family owned was to be left in the apartment for his brothers Mike and Tony and sister Vincenza, (Vincie,) who were starting their new lives in the city.

It was not generosity on Gabriel's part, rather a practical decision; Gabriel did not want to be bothered with moving anything. His short stay home was not even spent in the house. Gabriel went off to his hangouts and to see his cronies. And, having taken care of his own needs, he gave Pete some money, leaving the family to fend for themselves for the trip north. Gabriel was off again on the Washington Irving.

When the Cicales finally departed from NYC, the few possessions they took were mostly the clothing each owned. Pete's mother had some family photographs she clung to. Her children helped carry the wall pictures of Jesus, her other statues of the saints she believed in, and some knick knacks and canisters from the old country.

It was a very tearful time for Pete's mother. She was going to church to talk with the priest several times a day until their departure. This, she felt would give her the strength she needed to move on.

Pete planned on getting a horse and wagon to take them on their journey north. Pete did not drive, in NYC there was no need to. But, Pete realized he did not know the roads north yet, and no maps were available.

The hard packed dirt horse and carriage roads leading upstate were slowly being replaced for the new horseless carriages, the automobile. But all was at the beginning stages; a planned schematic diagram for a cohesive nationwide highway system would not be instituted for several decades, in the 1950s under President Eisenhower.

Pete had worried needlessly. When he was informed that there were no furnishings to move, the journey north became easier. With his father having gone on ahead, he'd be free to make the journey exciting for the family. They would not go the fancy way of Gabriel. Oh no, Gabriel was not going to spend that kind of money on them. They would take the train.

The locomotive rolled along the tracks heading north, and Pete was the guide. He shared his knowledge with the family; pointing out the foliage, the vast open spaces, the mountains, and the majestic homes. They ate sandwiches that were packed for the trip; no dining car here. He hoped that by the time they reached their new home, he would have created the enthusiasm necessary for this to be a positive move.

Pete realized he had too much to do; he could not worry about anything other than providing for them. He had no time to waste attending to each person's emotional state.

The arrival at the homestead was something to behold. The family descended from the horse and carriage that they had hired at the train depot. Pete's mother, his four sisters–Bridgette was the oldest at twenty-eight, Anna was eighteen, Elizabetta (called Bettina) was sixteen, Frankie was fifteen, Margaret was almost thirteen, and Pete who was already twenty-two, came up the path to the house. They were all wide-eyed, awkwardly glancing around, hugging on to their small treasures. This was their Ellis Island. In front of them was a vision as powerful as the Statue of Liberty was to new immigrants when they arrived on American shores.

They saw that the door of the house, the two story Dutch colonial indigenous to the valley since the seventeenth century, was wide open.

The house was white with a gambrel roof and overhanging eaves. The shutters were a vibrant green, accenting the beautiful oak tree that would shade parts of the house in the morning hours. The elegant porch was now filled with a glider, a large rocking chair, a wooden table and chairs, and several Adirondack chairs that are still in style today.

They stood dumbstruck; just a train ride away were the noises and crowding of the only world they had ever known. Here was this beautiful house surrounded by all this land that was now their home. Pete had tried to prepare them on the trip up, but seeing everything in person was an entirely different experience.

Pete looked over at his mother, she had her eyes closed. She was clasping her rosary beads. He knew she was praying and he was grateful for that.

Then a voice boomed out to them, "Io sono in casa. Entrare." (I am in the house. Come in.)

Of course it was Gabriel, calling out as if he were welcoming guests to the Mohonk Lodge.

They walked gingerly up the front steps and entered their new home. On the right, after entering the foyer, was their new living room; a sea of color, coordinated in dark burgundy and pink; the delicate patterned floral wallpaper, a mantled fireplace, a Victorian sofa, side tables, a brass floor lamp, and even an area rug over the stained dark oak wide floor board. The room was a beautiful decorative vision. And, sitting nonchalantly in a dark leather wing chair, his feet resting on the matching ottoman, was Gabriel. By his side sat a gallon of wine.

Pete remembered that his father had told him the house was completely empty. Now it looked as if someone had been living here for years. He was not surprised.

Gabriel was great at giving orders and Pete knew that he would have been a great taskmaster to have all this happen in such a short amount of time. Nothing was impossible where his father was concerned. Or, perhaps Gabriel had simply lied to him about the house having nothing in it; Pete had not been privy to any bank transactions. He had not been permitted to enter the private office there. Also, he did not see the inside of the house on his first trip there.

However it had happened, all the interior rooms were decorated to the hilt. A wood burning stove and an icebox were in place. There were dishes, pots, silverware, and all additional supplies required for cooking. Cross stitch table cloths with matching napkins were found too.

For the exterior buildings Gabriel had ordered everything that Pete had requested, such as the machinery, equipment, tools, and seedlings. He was finished. He could rest. It was now Pete's turn to make everything pay off.

Gabriel looked at this wife, Elizabetta, and said, "Ho fame," (I am hungry) and so a new life began.

Pete's mother and her daughters walked out of the living room, past the dining room to the kitchen at the back of the house. There was even a large kitchen table with wooden chairs, a far cry from the wooden planks that they had used to create a table out of their bath tub in NYC. The windows looked out to the summer kitchen, which was decorated as well. Farther out, they could see through the windows, the abundance of land and buildings surrounding the house; the mountains were a perfect faraway backdrop.

Everyone scrambled to make dinner. All the girls worked together to make Gabriel happy. There was no time for anyone to digest the enormity of this new life ahead of them. Soon the aromas of the sauce cooking permeated the house. They were home.

Later, after dinner, the family explored the rest of the interior rooms. All the floors were hardwood; all the walls had beautiful paper adorning them. No one would dare ask their father if they were that way when he purchased the home. And as usual, he volunteered no information.

To the left was a formal parlor, doubling as a music room. A piano, two burgundy settees, and large burgundy, pink and baby blue striped upholstered chairs were in that glorious room, quite elegant for the period; extraordinary for this family who had been living in almost squalor. Pete had none of these grand things on his list. Where did they come from?

Behind the living room on the right was the dining room, with an ornate table and chairs and a china cabinet with formal dinnerware and glasses. The women had passed it earlier on the way to the kitchen. This was where their first delicious meal had been eaten, for Gabriel had insisted they use the formal dining room that day.

The second floor contained four spacious bedrooms. Beds were in place with night stands and dressers. The girls had two bedrooms, the boys shared a room. The master bedroom was for the parents. In the upstairs bathroom was a large claw foot tub; a smaller bathroom was downstairs.

Behind the elaborate front hall staircase was another set of stairs. They led down to a cellar that was the length of the house, beneath the first floor. The dirt was made mostly of clay going up the walls and floor, compacted and leveled to a height of eight feet. There was a cistern in the middle used for the water supply. The roof of the cellar was made up of large hardwood unfinished 2x12 inch beams.

Twenty gallons of wine that Gabriel had purchased were already in the cellar, later to be replaced by gallons of wine that would come directly off his own land. Empty shelves lined the walls that would be filled with preserves. A dozen jars sat waiting to be filled.

The cellar was good for preserving. The earth would keep this area ten or fifteen degrees cooler than the rest of the house.

An outhouse stood behind the main house, still functioning, as the bathrooms of the 1920s were nothing like those of today.

Everything was so new. Evening came and it was too dark to walk the land. Pete knew that the entire family would come face-to-face with daily life on the farm soon enough. He personally had a huge endeavor before him.

For Pete nothing had changed except where he would work. Gabriel had packed in NYC and here he was. Pete had to become a farmer; he would have to make the farm work if the family was to survive in this new environment.

Chapter 6

PETE MEETS THE LAND

Pete hadn't closed his eyes all night. He had talked with Frankie until he heard the soft snoring of his younger brother. He waited as long as he could stand it, daybreak would come soon enough for the rest of the family, but Pete had to get a move on. He dressed in the dark, tiptoed down the stairs and out the door before anyone else was out of bed.

Today was the beginning of their new life. Each member of the family would be on his or her own, to learn more about their new home. Pete couldn't afford an ounce of concern about running the household. He had to put his focus on how he would work the land.

Pete opened the front door, the sun came up on the horizon, and he breathed in and took his first positive step onto the property. His mission was to see where the machinery and tools had been put. Pete had planned it all in his head. He had learned a great deal from the farmers who were now his neighbors. Gabriel had kept his word and delivered, everything was in place to get him started, just as Pete had requested.

There was a large wagon by the side of the house; a stone boat was sitting right next to it. Pete had learned about this transport device when he had visited the Locamente family. Joe had shown him one and Pete had drawn a picture in his notebook, the book he had given to his father.

There it was, low to the ground with wide board flooring. Two round pieces of wood laid under the large wooden planks, called skids. The stone boat looked like a sleigh, standing no more than twelve inches high. Pete knew that the stone boat was a necessity for the farm for he would need it to pick up rocks of all sizes on the property. He was aware that something was missing: a horse to pull it.

One of the buildings he entered had all his tools carefully hung: hammers, saws of all types, (especially interesting were the two sided ones), axes, picks, shovels, hoes, rakes. Pete was busy examining his new tools when he heard the noise of approaching wagons.

He came out of the shed and stood watching as the large wagons came into view, pulled by four horses. Two older men had arrived to deliver the livestock. On the first wagon Pete saw his horses. The men knew exactly what they were doing. They unloaded and brought the livestock into the barns.

Angelo, the shorter of the two spoke to Pete. "Am sure ya were spectin these. Your pa told us to giv em to ya. Pete yer name, right? I'm Angelo, this here is my brotha, Tony."

The men were an answer to Pete's prayers, for not only did they deliver the livestock and their equipment, but they also gave Pete an instant course on how to work the animals for the farm. Then, they departed just as quickly as they had come.

Pete walked the barn area to meet his new livestock. There were chickens, sheep, a dairy cow, and three small pigs. Pete talked to each of them, and patted them down. Pete then walked over to his old horses, two plugs named Tom and Jerry. He was telling them the rules of the road, and within a half hour the man and all his animals had bonded. The latter knew who their new master was, and it was to become a strong and satisfactory relationship.

He came back to reality when he heard in the distance the beautiful and special sound of a voice he loved so much.

"Viene qui Pietro."(Come here Peter.) His mother was calling him in for breakfast.

Pete responded quickly. He always did for her. On his walk back to the house, Pete counted many trees along the path that he'd have to cut and clear. He also spotted large patches of barren land. He knew he'd have to remove the rocks and boulders to cultivate the land.

Pete had only walked a small area of the vast property. It would take a lot more time than he had just spent for him to survey the entire parcel. He'd have to configure all the land to make it as profitable as possible for his future crops.

He had a million things on his mind as he entered the house and smelled the breakfast cooking on the stove.

At the kitchen table were all his siblings, laughing and enjoying themselves.

Bridgette, was one of two born in the old country. Mike, who had stayed in NYC, was the other. She didn't talk much, was very old school, and had always looked elderly. She was generally quiet and humble, but she seemed happy that morning.

Anna, was the boisterous one. She was laughing heartily when Pete entered the room.

Bettina, was generally quiet but was known in the family as strong willed. She was "chomping at the bit" to ask Pete questions about their new home.

Frankie, was holding court with his sisters. He was a chameleon. He could be serious or a prankster. But most important, Frankie had an amazing creative talent. He could do almost anything with his hands. Soon, he would even be able to play the piano and so many other instruments at family gatherings... and all self-taught.

The youngest at the table was little Margaret, who was "quiet as a church mouse." She was the observer at family functions.

Pete's mother was laughing too. She was actually sitting at the table talking to her children. Pete had never seen this before in their small tenement apartment, for they always had to be quiet when their father was around. But this morning Gabriel was upstairs sleeping. The house was so large that no one worried about disturbing him. He was unable to hear the noise emanating from downstairs.

There were so many things that each wanted to talk about. Pete was content to grin that infectious smile, knowing this would be his only respite for the day. His siblings directed questions at him and he answered assuredly. He knew he was major miles from achievement of any kind, but he was the man at the table.

The days went quickly after that. There was so much to do. He kept busy morning to nightfall, never stopping. This was to be his life and he embraced the challenges. Pete found his true place in life. He loved the soil.

In my youth, when Dad and I worked the fields, he would often pick up the soil, smell it and hand it to me. I can hear his *Peteism* now, as he would say, "Son, feel the earth. God is in the soil. When you feel the soil in your hands you know that God is present." It was a powerful statement spoken by a wise man.

Pete set up a long and tedious plan to succeed at farming. First, he used the stone boat to remove the rocks and boulders. Tom and Jerry, the horses, pulled that low sleigh along as Pete, with Frankie helping, piled all the rocks out of the way. They brought all those stones to the end of the property, setting them up as a free standing wall to act as a boundary line.

Next, the problem trees were cut down with a two-sided saw. The branches were burned; the trunks were cut up for firewood and piled up on the side of the house not far from the back door. In the winter months they would need the wood to heat the fireplace in the house.

Pete worked hard, his skin toughened from the elements. He was already muscular from all his manual labor in NYC, but now his muscles had muscles. His body was chiseled and that tanned leathery look stayed with him for the rest of his life. He had filled out from the fresh country air and this boy was becoming a handsome looking man.

Pete finally had the land cleared and ready for plowing. The land had to be cultivated. The horses and plough were used to turn over the land. The plough would go down a foot to dig up all the root systems from the trees that had just been cut down. Those roots would have interfered with the planting process. A harrow (a frame with spikes or sharp-edged discs) was attached to the horses to break up the remaining roots and weeds, preparing the soil for planting.

Frankie had an acumen that was a complement to Pete's. He did not like the manual labor involved with farming, but he helped Pete in another way. He was naturally adept at working with mechanical things. Although he had no formal training, today Frankie would be considered a mechanical engineer. He loved to tinker and invent things; actually having an innate gift for this. Frankie would contribute by fixing up the barns and sheds, fixing the foundation, screening for the summer kitchen, building cabinets, anything that required ingenuity of that nature.

Pete had the heaviest work done. The land was cleared. From then on, he would run the farm with his mother, the only other person in the family who worked as hard as him. Elizabetta was a female version of Pete. Until the day she died, all his mother did was work.

Together they would plant crops that spring for harvesting in the fall. Pete and his mother planted fruits and vegetables that would grow quickly, providing necessities for the family. They added to those a large quantity of the same kind of fast growing produce to sell for profit.

The farm could not become an instant success. Pete did exactly what he had learned. He made mistakes, corrected them, and kept going. The goal would be to have a productive and lucrative farm; in time the years would subsequently reward them with apples, grapes, and off season crops for them to eat and sell.

Pete hated the fact that his mother had to work so hard, but there was no one else to step up to the plate. In fact, she actually enjoyed being with her son, believing there was nothing they couldn't do if they worked together.

Elizabetta completely loved Pete. She continued to take Gabriel's physical and verbal abuse, as long as Pete was there to defend her and act as a buffer. Pete did not sit passively when his father started ranting. He was never disrespectful; however, he did stand between his father and mother, staring Gabriel down. Gabriel would then back off. He knew his limits when it came to Pete, the mule. He didn't dare "fire" Pete for insubordination. Gabriel knew he needed him to do the work, and that is exactly what Pete did, day in and day out, never once complaining.

The apple seedlings would become the family's main staple. However they would take a long time to become productive. The trees would take up to seven years to earn money for the family. Still, it was a wise investment, for those trees would then produce apples for decades; as long as they were cared for correctly.

Pete and Elizabetta planted the vineyards for the grapes. Pete had located an area at the back of the property that already had a large section with grape vines. He just added to it. The grape vines that Pete had found were mature. Normally grapes would take ten years to produce a decent crop. The good news was that the vines could last up to 100 years. That would be an instant crop for the family. There were concord and zinfandel grapes.

Gabriel ordered Frankie to make large wooden casks for 500 gallons of wine that he would drink yearly by himself. The rest could be picked and sold after he took his allotment, bringing an instant return for the family. The newer grape seedlings would need time before a crop could be harvested.

The grapes had to be sprayed to prevent fungus, a powdery mildew that could form on the leaves, stems and grapes, black rot that could appear as circular lesions on the leaves, or insects that could destroy the crops.

Frankie devised a sprayer using a tank that would hold 300 gallons of water. An insecticide was mixed into the tank as well. The water was pumped into the tank from a nearby brook that ran along the farm. Frankie rigged a hose, adding a screen to the end of it. The other part was connected to a motor that, when started, pulled the water through the hose and into the tank to be filled. Frankie also made a spray gun.

Pete walked behind the sprayer while Frankie drove along the rows with a small Caterpillar D2 that had slow moving tracks. Pete would turn on the nozzle and shoot 275 lbs. of pressure at the plants. This made Pete's job so much easier. Pete also had to make sure the grape vines were spaced properly so that the clusters received equal sunlight. He checked often to trim down the bottom stems, keeping the vines healthy.

The sprayer invention was good for the grapes, but was even better for the apples that Pete and his mother had planted: McIntosh, Red Delicious, and Cortland apple varieties. Those crops had to be sprayed 15-20 times each growing season. Frankie's invention was a lifesaver in attacking all the problems that could destroy the apple crops.

Meanwhile, to survive, as I said earlier, they planted seasonal crops: the strawberries, raspberries, blueberries, blackberries, and currants that would give them immediate income. All the plants had to be fertilized by hand, a back bending chore, but a necessity if the crop was to be healthy.

The cherry trees would take several years to develop – Windsors and Bings were planted. Peaches and pears (Bartlett and Clapp) also would be slow to mature.

It would all take time but Pete was methodical in his care, and each experience made him more proficient.

While all this work was going on, yonder under a tree, Gabriel was resting, just as he had planned. He had quickly found his favorite tree and drank his gallon of wine each day that he had originally purchased from local farmers. But, soon the wine was made from the fruit of his son's labor; grapes from the family vineyard, with a raw onion a day, grown from their own garden.

Pete's sisters tried to help with the cooking and cleaning. They also tried to stay invisible. Gabriel did not like the way they cooked, so Pete's mom claimed that chore too. She did all this while praying a great deal, feeling there was no other way to make it through the long days.

When I asked Dad how he did it, he simply replied, "I used common sense." This was another *Peteism*, he often told me, "Use common sense, son. I'll take that over education any day of the week." He said, "If I'm book smart and have no common sense, then I wouldn't know a lick about what to do when I hit the street."

Pete worked seven days a week from sunup to sundown, coming in from the fields only to eat and sleep.

Time went quickly. One season followed another and the routine of farming became just that, a routine. Pete's job was to work the farm and that was all he did. The years moved along. Pete took his time; he wanted to do everything correctly.

My dad taught me the lessons of the first days on the farm as he lived his entire life, something that was hard to understand or even live by, especially when I was young.

His *Peteism* in this case was, "Son, pace yourself. Life is like a creeper gear on a tractor. Go slow and learn from your mistakes. As you learn, increase your gear. If you go too fast, you will miss what is around you. Going a little bit slower will allow you to learn correctly."

I know this lesson. I am sure you know it too. So, why don't we follow it?

Chapter 7

THE COURTSHIP

The Great Depression hit. It affected the entire country. The Cicales in the city felt it as did those in the country. But the country Cicales had something so many others did not. They had the land and it was a meal ticket for the whole family. They could live off their own produce, their own animals, the milk of their cows.

They sold their produce to the outside markets though few had money to buy. The family had always lived on a tight budget, so not much changed. They just kept plodding along. Pete learned how to utilize his time. None of his day was wasted.

Time helped the seedlings grow into productive trees. Experimentation followed and the experience of success, proper fertilization, harvesting, packing, shipping and preserving for long winters all helped to create a self- sustaining life.

The years passed quickly. The seeds sown started to reap the harvest. The family did the same. Everyone was growing up, forming life relationships and moving on. Pete watched as it all took place. He was not a participant. He was a farmer. He had responsibility to boot.

The large family grew larger and larger. As the farm started to produce its bumper crop, so had the family members who had started to spread their wings.

The first to get married was Bridgette. She was the first of those who had come up to the farm to leave the fold. She stayed in the area, married, and had two boys. Unfortunately, her husband died young and Pete felt another responsibility. Throughout his life he looked after her and her children.

The other siblings joined the marriage brigade. Those in the city married; those in the country did likewise. Marriage and children flowed freely from the prolific siblings. Vincie was the only girl to stay in the city. She had the most children, ten.

Weddings, children, baptisms, birthdays; anything that could bring the family together was happily anticipated. The holidays were particularly joyous times when the family from NYC came to visit those who had moved to the farm.

The summers in the outdoor kitchen, or winters in the music room brought sounds of laughter, lots of noisy children, and the sweet harmony of the singing Cicales. As I mentioned before, Frankie taught himself to play many musical instruments: guitar, piano, banjo, and accordion. Frankie could change his persona from engineer to musician, to prankster to rascal in a blink.

The siblings sang the Italian songs of their parents' and the popular songs of the times. They subsequently taught them to their children who in turn passed them down to theirs. The Van Trapps had nothing on the Cicales. The only difference was, the Cicales did not take the act on the road.

Life had its discords, just like all families. There were fights among the siblings. Some disappeared for a few years. Others did not want to see their father, Gabriel, the person who had hurt them so much.

After Bridgette, Anna and Bettina married, some of the siblings met at their homes. Pete always brought their mother to see them. She was still their world. She did not say much, but it hurt her that they chose to meet elsewhere. Home to her was where she and their father lived. However, she was used to doing what appeased and did what was asked.

Family gatherings were often organized whenever Gabriel took off for awhile. No one asked where he went. They were happiest when he was not around to remind them of the bullying of their youth.

Even little Margaret married, leaving Pete and Frankie the only siblings left on the farm. Pete's mother helped out, but Pete did most of the work. He was now thirty-three years old.

There was a young woman who lived in a farmhouse less than a mile down the road. Although she was almost twelve years younger than Pete, she had noticed him years before. She would often take walks past the farm, catching glimpses of this handsome, hardworking man. Now and then he noticed her. But Pete was a shy man who didn't know the first thing about courting.

One day though, he mentioned something to his mother about the young woman:

"Mi piace la signorina,"(I like the young lady.)

"Che?" (Who?) his mother was intrigued.

"Signorina Caterina Porpiglia."

"Parlare con Papa," (Speak with Papa) and Pete, who needed a few reminders from his mother, finally did just that.

Pete approached his father apprehensively, "Voglio essere introdotti a Caterina Porpiglia."(I want to be introduced to Caterina Porpiglia.)

His father replied in his broken dialect, "Parlero con il padre."(I will speak with her father.)

Both men, Dominick Porpiglia, the father of Caterina, and Gabriel Cicale, Pete's father, had met many years before in the boarding house in New Paltz. It was a given that all the families of Milton knew each other. They all attended St. James Church. All of Pete's siblings made their own matches, but Pete was so reticent that he did not have the first idea of how to go about it.

Caterina was Dominick's oldest child. She was also the most interested in learning; but don't tell that to her three sisters – Angie, Grace, and Fanny, or her brothers - Tony, Pete and Joe.

Caterina was an old soul, born with powerful instincts. She was a big girl, not overweight, but also not someone who would be called petite or girly, who had grown into a full bodied woman. Her face was part of her character. She looked at you when she spoke; did not back down from interacting. The only thing that hindered her was her eyesight. She was actually legally blind. She needed glasses that were as thick as coke bottles. When young, at school, she would take the glasses off. A famous often repeated saying was, "No one makes passes at girls who wear glasses."

Schooling was easy for Caterina. She always sat in the front of the classroom and followed the movement of the hand of the teacher as she wrote on the chalkboard. She memorized everything. Her acumen was beyond belief when it came to numbers. She could add anything in her head. She had wanted to become further educated, but as it was with most families who were hit by the Depression, she went to work instead in a packing plant as a bookkeeper.

Her attractiveness was based on her good heart, her strong religious beliefs, and her ability to help take care of others. She, like Pete, spoke Italian with her parents, who were immigrants from Sicily. She was old-fashioned. She dressed that way, thought that way, and was a dutiful child. When Gabriel came to their farm and asked Dominick, for her hand in marriage to his son, her father could have simply said, "Yes."

However, Dominick was an entirely different kind of man from Gabriel. He was a wonderful person, kind, thoughtful, strong, and loving; the antithesis of Gabriel. Caterina was the rock of the Porpiglia family. Her father and mother adored her. He turned to his daughter, who would soon turn twenty-four years of age, and told her that it was her decision to make.

Kate's family had an entirely different life in New York City than the Cicales. Her father had taken the family up to the country due to changes in NYC, brought on by Prohibition. The Cosa Nostra was putting more of a stranglehold on small business in NYC, by demanding their cut on the action.

Dominick was an honorable man. His family loved him, his friends, neighbors and associates all felt the warmth he exuded. He had class. The difference between the two fathers was that Dominick was a born worker; he had a very successful pool hall in NYC. Dominick was making almost $1500.00 a week when he decided NYC was no longer a safe place to raise a family and moved his wife and children to Milton. He became an apple farmer, quite successful at that, in spite of the Depression and the rest of the hardships of the time.

As a point of interest, his son Joe's children are among the largest apple producers in the state of New York, as of this writing.

Caterina was excited by the prospect of marrying Pete Cicale. She had walked past the Cicale farm often, hoping that Pete would notice her. She knew of his work ethic, his responsibility for his family, his love of his mother, his decency, his demeanor – as it was known by all in the valley – for Milton was a small town. She thought of the strong, muscular, handsome, physical man, Peter Cicale, and said softly to her father, "Vieni con me, Papa."(Come with me Papa.)

Dominick excused himself and walked inside with his daughter. "Quale la vostra decision, mia cara?" (What is your decision, my dear?)

"Si, Papa. Voglio sposare Pietro Cicale." (Yes, Papa, I want to marry Peter Cicale.)

Father and daughter walked back outside. He told Gabriel Cicale that his daughter had agreed to the marriage. The courtship could now begin.

The courtship was far from ordinary, even by today's standards. The age gap between the two was never apparent, for Mom was 23, looking 34; Dad, a bashful man of 34 years looked 23. He had left his fate regarding marriage to his father. He was a respectful son and no one would have expected anything different.

Pete came to call and the now engaged twosome had to get to know each other. As it would be for their whole life together, Caterina initiated the talking and pulled Pete into conversation.

They took long walks through the countryside. They talked about growing up. She was from Little Italy, he from Italian Harlem. Both had come to the country from the city. Both came from large families. Both had assumed control of taking care of others. The differences were primarily in the way they were raised.

Caterina came from a loving family. Her parents showed great warmth and love for their children.

Pete had the love of his mother. His father was another story. Pete did not say anything negative about his father. Nor did he have to. Gabriel's wanton reputation was a well known tale spread all over the town. In fact, Pete never said a bad word about anyone.

One time Pete took Kate (as he came to call her) to a movie. She was all excited and moved in closer to Pete as the lights went out and the movie began. Pete did not catch the hint. She tried to whisper to him. He didn't get it. He looked straight ahead at the screen. The movie ended and they exited the theatre.

Kate reached over and took Pete's hand. He was shocked, oblivious to the progressive stages of courting. She began chatting away about the movie, "Wasn't the story wonderful? It was so romantic. Don't you just love Clark Gable?"

Pete stuttered an answer, "Y-Yeah, it was really nice."

Kate knew that she had to be more aggressive. When they came back to her parent's home, she pointed to the porch swing. "Come, Pete, please sit here, next to me?" and motioned a spot for him.

She cuddled next to him. The courtship had been going on awhile; they were almost married and not much affection had taken place.

"Don't you want to kiss me?" She offered.

"Sure I do," Pete replied, staring straight ahead.

"Well then, just do it," and she leaned forward.

Pete turned and gave her a small peck on the cheek. This was going nowhere, so Kate just pulled his face toward her and taught Pete what a kiss really meant. She had never done that before, but she knew what she wanted and by golly she was going to get it.

"That was nice," Pete said. And then finally getting the message, he kissed her the way it should be done.

This was not going to be a passionless marriage. He just needed to get out of creeper gear.

The courtship grew warmer. Pete was building a house on the Cicale homestead, a place to bring his bride. It was not a big house, just 600 square feet. Frankie helped him, for building was his forte.

In fact, Frankie was starting to do more and more work in the area, building homes, remodeling; all things that he could do so easily with his skilled hands.

Pete took time out of every work day to build his "wedding house." He worked as quickly as possible, for that was the only obstacle to proceeding with the nuptials. It took six months before it was finally finished.

Now, Pete could marry Caterina.

Chapter 8

PETE AND CATERINA MARRY

The wedding was a splendid affair, taking place on October 28, 1939. Dominick gave away his oldest child in style.

Caterina wore the most dazzling wedding dress, a demure lace high neck gown, pulled in tight at the waist. It then flowed out with yards and yards of hand embroidered lace, a long flowing train, and a beautiful matching headpiece.

The ceremony was held at St. James Church. The place would play a key role in their entire lives. St. James, in Milton, New York, was the church where they were married, worshipped, would baptize and confirm their future children, and finally the services for their deaths would be conducted there.

Although Caterina was the center of attention at this lavish affair, the rest of the bridal party looked lovely as well. She was attended by five: the Maid of Honor was her sister Angie; bridesmaids were Pete's sisters and her sister, Gracie. Pete had five attendants as well: the Best Man was his brother, Frankie. His groomsmen were Kate's brother Tony, a friend, Joe, Cousin Goggs, and two other cousins.

The wedding reception took place at Friedman's Shady Lawn Rest Hotel, a place frequented by tourists, especially in the summer months. The hotel was built in 1805, and was one of the oldest hotels in Ulster County.

Friedman's had a little sordid history associated with it. Doesn't everything? In the 1930s during Prohibition, Jack "Legs" Diamond, aka Gentleman Jack, one of the most famous Irish-American racketeers, used the hotel as his headquarters. He was muscling his way into the bootlegging business. One night while playing cards with two of the guests, Gentleman Jack discovered that they were actually federal agents, who were looking to arrest him. A gunfight ensued. Legs escaped and hid in Albany, farther upstate. Rival bootleggers eventually found him there and shot him down. This story added to the desirability of the hotel. Everyone wanted to go where something a little shady took place.

The hotel did not last as Friedman's. Shortly after the wedding, it closed down, not to reopen for almost fifteen years, when it became the Rocking Horse Dude Ranch, which is still in existence today

Enough about the place, the reception was something else. It was not your usual football style wedding – sandwiches, beer, and large buffet – rather, a full sit-down dinner at the hotel about four miles from the church. The newlyweds were driven from the church to the reception in style; her dad's 1939 Packard trailing tin cans and old shoes tied to the back bumper.

When Kate walked into the reception as Mrs. Cicale, the top lace gown had been removed. A satin form fitting sleeveless dress, a look favored by the film sirens of the day, was revealed. Kate looked beautiful, not a word used often to describe her looks; but that was her day and she shined like the brightest star in the universe. She was extremely happy.

There were 250 guests at the affair. The best photographer from the area took the pictures. Dominick paid for everything. Gabriel did not even consider contributing – he only paid for things that gave him pleasure, or benefited him.

Mr. and Mrs. Cicale went on a two week honeymoon to Niagara Falls and Washington D.C. It was the first vacation for both of them. Although the relationship was a little strained before the marriage, for no other reason than Pete's shyness during the courtship, they came back from that honeymoon with an accord, built as solid as cement. Both knew that this was a lifelong relationship. They would work together for almost 47 years, each determined to make the other stronger and better.

Dad didn't say much about that day; but he did recite a *Peteism*: "Son, be content within your own body, and your choices in life. I am, and was on my wedding day." Somehow I believe that surmises who he was.

The bride and groom
Catherine and Peter Cicale

Wedding of Caterina and Peter Cicale
October 29, 1939

50th wedding anniversary, Gabriel and Elizabetta Cicale
With 7 of their 9 children

Before the honeymoon, Pete and Catherine
Dressed to go off to Niagara Falls

Pete and Catherine on honeymoon, 1939

Pete – Original House 1941

Chapter 9

A FAMILY IS BORN

Dad moved his bride into the little 600 square foot house that he had built with his own hands. Over the years he called mom by so many names: Caterina, Kate, Catherine, and Kay. But his favorite quip was always this: "Ain't it, Kay?" It was his way of getting her Good Housekeeping Seal of Approval for everything that was to happen in their lives.

They instinctively knew their roles. Dad was the worker; Mom was in charge of everything else, never showing that she was to anyone other than her husband. She knew her place; he knew his, and together it worked out well.

She fixed up their little house, made it warm and cozy. She was a great cook and loved to please him.

He went out to the fields early in the day. He came in for lunch and then went back outside until dark.

And so they began their life together; even meals were defined from the beginning. Early in their marriage, Pete came in to the kitchen to find Catherine had made a sandwich of baloney and cheese for his lunch.

He blinked his eyes in disbelief and said, "I don't eat sandwiches. This is not lunch." He thrust his forefinger at the plate before him. "I want hot food. You don't serve that to a working man."

"What do you want, spaghetti every day?"

"No, I want a hot meal. But I do want my spaghetti every Wednesday and Sunday."

Catherine had no problem making her husband happy. She stayed on at her job with Nardone's Cooling, a packing house for produce, as long as the hours did not interfere with her duties and responsibility as head of the Cicale household.

She also helped her husband with his book-keeping, hiring of migrant workers for the harvest, sorting, packing, and general accounting.

In the years to follow, Catherine became the sole voice of the household, especially when dealing with the selling of the crops and dealing with the buyers who were to come up from NYC. Her role became the most important, financially speaking, in keeping things together. Pete knew that she was much stronger in regard to all aspects of running the farm, except for physically working it. But she even pitched in there too, whenever she was needed.

Times were tough for Catherine, living on the farm with her one particular in-law. Catherine loved Pete's mother, Elizabetta, but strongly disliked his father, Gabriel. Kate knew her place and for the most part, she just tried to make life easier for her husband's mother.

However, there came a time when Gabriel tried to raise his hand to Pete's mom. Catherine walked right up and stood between them, glaring at the man. Pete came running. Together, husband and wife let him know in no uncertain terms that they were always going to defend Pete's mother. Gabriel wisely backed off. He retreated to his tree, eating his raw onion, and drinking his wine.

He never attempted to go after Elizabetta again in his son or his son's wife's presence. What happened inside the house at other times no one knows? And Elizabetta certainly never told. But Kate now knew why Pete could never leave his mother. She took it upon herself to keep a watchful eye on the situation from then on.

Kate also learned from the very beginning of their marriage that she was not to talk about Gabriel in a derogatory fashion. Pete knew his father well; now so did Catherine. However, Gabriel was his father, and that was that.

Pete loved his small house where his married life began. Frankie, now twenty-seven, was still living at the big house. He was never around though. Frankie had started his own contracting firm, working on other farms, remodeling and building. He also worked on the commercial buildings of the area and the churches. He was instinctively good at all he did.

When World War II came, Pete was too old to be drafted; besides he had responsibilities that involved several people. But Pete always regretted that he was too young for the First World War, and too old for the second. Frankie was also too old by this time; he was classified as head of the family farm and the support of his parents, although technically Pete was in charge of the farm.

The day came when Frankie realized he was in love. He had met Mary, a divorcee from Greenwich Village on Sullivan Street in NYC, when she had come to visit family in the Hudson Valley. Mary, who already had a young daughter, was considered a "used woman," and not a good person by many in the community, for divorce was unheard of in the Cicale family. What kind of woman would marry; have a child, then divorce? But, Frankie who had dated several girls from the area knew that Mary was the one.

Frankie said to Pete, "I am in love and I don't care what the rest of the family says."

He had to figure out a way to court her. Frankie could not afford to go by ferry or train to NYC. At a junkyard he found: a frame, an engine, four tires, a ripped up interior; all parts of what was once a 1931 Ford. He bought the whole kit and caboodle for $5.00. Little by little he found more parts, fixed it up, and actually got it to run.

Thus, his courtship with Mary grew, as he drove back and forth to NY along 9W. She became his wife in 1944, a marriage that lasted for 60 years.

The family was not happy with his choice. Frankie did not care. One of his sisters said, "She is a whore, and the little girl is a bastard."

In those days, those were the kind of words used for women who were divorced with a child. During that time, she was not only scorned, but cursed at in Italian. Some of the sisters even threw rocks at her.

Catherine saw what was happening and immediately came to Mary's defense. She warned the sisters-in-law, "Leave Mary alone. This is Frankie's wife." She protected her from any family negativity and Catherine and Mary became the best of friends over the years.

Pete couldn't get involved in the petty bickering. He was a live and let live guy. "Mary is fine, she is

Frankie's wife," he let his sisters know. He and Mary developed a good relationship too. He loved his brother, period.

Catherine was an intelligent sweet woman, unless provoked. She became the family protector, a buffer who helped keep harmony. But when she got her horns twisted, watch out. She was a Scorpio and boy could she sting if she felt it was necessary.

Dad would say to me, "I wouldn't like to be the one who is on the wrong side of a disagreement with your mom. You don't stand a chance of winning."

In September of 1940 their first child, a girl, was born. She was named after the mother Pete loved so well. Elizabeth was a welcome addition to the family. Catherine became a full-time wife and mother after the birth, giving up her job at Nardone's.

Elizabeth was the first grandchild for the Porpiglias, Mom's side of the family. She was only eight years younger than their youngest child, Joe. She was born in Vassar Hospital in Poughkeepsie. She was a large baby, 10 lbs. 2 oz., yet as an adult the smallest of the three children Pete and Catherine Cicale were to have.

Elizabeth, free spirited, never really tried to communicate with either set of grandparents, she didn't learn Italian, the primary language for the elder generation. She was an individual who was not really interested in family history or language.

I came next, named Gabriel. Mom, ever the businesswoman, wasn't about to let the $500.00 given for my name slip away. It helped my parents get through a lean time. They used it to fix one of the tractors. They could never say I was worth nothing.

I was born in the house, on the kitchen table, delivered by a midwife, Rosie Lofaro, who died at 104 years of age. She was a second cousin, who delivered many children in the Hudson Valley. I weighed in at 12 lbs. 2 oz., the highest number the produce scale went up to. So maybe it was a little more.

I was born busy, asking a million questions from the day I started talking, learning Italian, and loving visits with my Nonno and Nonna Porpiglia.

I, the first grandson, was treated like royalty. I loved being with them, thrived on the food of my heritage, and the excitement of just following them around wherever they went. I learned so much: how to cook, how to drive a tractor at two years of age, how to take bites of all the food that was cooling on the table. Of course, I did that when no one was looking. My maternal grandparents let me get away with murder, so I wanted to stay there more and more.

However, life would now take a different turn; the worst thing that would ever happen to Pete and his young family was about to happen. No one was prepared for what was about to unfold.

Chapter 10

THE BETRAYAL

I'm sure life appeared normal to all outsiders. It was internally, at the homestead, that things were about to change dramatically. Pete noticed it first.

His mother started to slow down. She didn't want to, she fought to hide it, but her son who had lived so much of his life with her as his central figure saw it, and was concerned.

He talked to Catherine. She too became alarmed and together they decided to get her to the doctor. There was no need to talk it over with Gabriel; her slowing down did not affect him yet. He would react only when his lifestyle became directly impacted.

Elizabetta was almost seventy-six years old. That was a full life in the early 1940s. If you think about how hard she worked, how many children she raised, the abuse she took from her husband, Elizabetta had to have had a strong constitution to be going to the doctor for one of the first times in her life at that age. The news was grave; she had cancer.

Pete's mother did not want anyone to know. She wanted to continue working as if nothing was the matter. Catherine, a very strong woman when necessary, asserted herself and notified the family. Her children and grandchildren were so incredibly sad. Elizabetta was their rock.

The only one who did not show a deep sense of sorrow was Gabriel. What a surprise! Unknown to all the family, he started making plans for the next stage of his life after his wife would die. After all, he had to continue to live. Who would cook and serve him his meals, help with the farm work, do the laundry? The man continued to live in his own egotistical world. He had to worry about himself.

The news came suddenly–a fait accompli–the farm was sold. WHAT? Yes, that was exactly what happened. Mr. Batista, an Italian immigrant who was moving his family north and was looking at property, had bought the homestead.

You'll never guess who told Mr. Batista about the farm; good ole Rosie, the boarding house owner in New Paltz, who had never lost touch with Gabriel. This was not really a surprise. He went to see her at the time that his wife became ill. She was told to confidentially put out feelers to see if anyone was interested in buying the farm.

When Mr. Batista went with Rosie to see the farm, Gabriel surreptitiously had them come when the entire family was at a baptism.

Gabriel went and sold all the land, the big house and to emphasize how little he cared for anyone but himself, he even sold the little house that Dad had built with his own hands for us. Everything Dad had worked for had been sold right out from under him. Our family had to vacate the property within four months.

Dad's brothers and sisters were very upset, but the direct impact would be on Dad, the one who had sacrificed every aspect of his life to serve his family.

Dad now had no home for his family, no land, and no job. But he accepted this quietly. Gabriel, as usual, offered no explanation as to why he was throwing his son and family off the property. Dad did not expect one. Mom was furious, but Dad would not let her verbally attack his father. There was quiet tension in their home.

Mr. Batista was put into Dad's hands. Pete was supposed to show Mr. Batista his property, the entire working farm. How ironic. Dad, who was losing everything, was to escort Mr. Batista around. Dad did not think about whether he should or shouldn't do this. His mother was still alive. And he would not defy his father.

So Dad took Mr. Batista for a tour of his new place. He spent several days helping the man acclimate to his purchase. Mr. Batista met a gentleman in Dad. Pete did not discuss what was happening to his world. He was losing all that he had devoted his life to. However, Mr. Batista was a very astute man. It did not take him long to figure out that Pete was getting the shaft, and he could not live with that. He approached Gabriel and suggested that they work the sale in a way that Pete could keep a parcel of land and his home. Gabriel was simply not interested. He basically told Mr. Batista the deal was done – the end.

Mr. Batista could not fathom the idea that a man would do this to his own flesh and blood. In the very short time he had been with Dad, he knew what an honorable man he was.

Mr. Batista said to Pete, "I want to give you a present of thirty-nine acres for you and your family to farm. I know your father is leaving you with nothing and did not make preparations for your family."

Dad said, "Thank you, sir, but I do not accept charity. I will figure something out for my family." Dad was a proud man and Mr. Batista was not surprised by his answer.

"Think about it, talk to your wife. I am sure I can help you."

Dad said, "I will talk with her and thank you for your kindness," knowing that he would tell Kate, but she would not change his mind.

Dad had a long talk with mom. She was the realist in the family. There were two small children involved; I was less than two years old. All Dad had done in his adult life was farming.

She knew how to handle Dad and suggested, "Go see Mr. Batista and offer to buy the piece of land, not just take it. We can pay him off over a few years."

That satisfied Dad. He went to see the new owner.

Mr. Batista was only too happy with that kind of arrangement. He said, "I have no problem with that, but you must live in your original home until you can build a new one on the land that you will now own. Okay?"

"Okay." Dad did not show the relief, but he certainly felt it. Mr. Batista knew he would get a good and helpful neighbor living next door to him. Dad knew that he had made a fair deal. A verbal agreement between the two men allowed my father to purchase the land from Mr. Batista and pay him back over time. They agreed on a price of $5,000.00 for the almost forty acres.

There was no contract drawn up. It was all done on a handshake, the same handshake that would dictate Dad's entire life. Dad paid Mr. Batista back in less than five years. He was finally a landowner.

A *Peteism* from that time and the subsequent experiences that followed in his life was this: "Shake a person's hand. Use a strong handshake to show that you have strong character. Then keep your word based on that handshake."

Elizabetta passed away; she never knew what had happened. The family had decided not to tell her. This deeply religious woman did not deserve to hear this kind of news on her deathbed.

Everyone mourned; oh I forgot, almost everyone mourned. Gabriel was planning his next move, a trip to Italy. He did manage to stick around for the funeral before leaving the very next day.

Chapter 11

BEGINNING AGAIN

Dad was extremely sad about her passing, yet relieved that his mother never found out what her husband had done. Dad never missed a payment to Mr. Batista and built another home for his family on the far end of the land.

He built it quickly, feeling an unwarranted obligation to vacate the original house that was now owned by Mr. Batista. This time it was a home of about 975 square feet, never really finished. The house was built of concrete blocks with three bedrooms and one bath. It is still standing there today. Dad worked so hard at farming that he had no time to do the things necessary to finish projects around the house. It took decades for him to cover the concrete blocks with stucco, and decades more to cover the stucco with aluminum siding. But our family had a home; the provider had come through again.

As a child growing up in this small town, I was embarrassed by the unfinished house. I would have the bus driver drop me off down the road from our home so that the other kids would not see that we still had raw stucco covering the place. "I'm so sorry, Dad, for my shallow bullshit. That house was a palace. Just want you to know that. I hope you can hear me long distance."

Dad, who had little formal education, knew that the limited size of our property would not be enough to provide for his family. He would have to figure out a way to supplement this income. He would use his common sense to get the family through again, but for the present time, land awaited him. First things first, Dad had to take care of the acreage that now belonged to him.

That may sound easy, but the new land that Pete owned was mostly barren. He dug in again. There was some areas of smaller produce, some grape vines; the larger crops that would create a real living for his family had to be started from scratch.

Pete began planting his apple, cherry, and pear trees that would all take years to give him a return on his time and investment. He worked hard, even building a barn at the back of the property for tractors, work horses, chickens, pigs, sheep, goats, cows, and a small area set up for the limited packing that would be done. This was not 400 acres, it was one tenth that. The work would be just as difficult because the original homestead had already survived and thrived through it's growing pains.

Dad's life was starting anew again. The only advantage was that he was now an experienced farmer. He still had to take things slow; he had to cultivate, plant and await the maturation process that only time could bring. What would he do in the meantime?

Making matters worse, winter was coming; there was no crop to plant. My father was having difficulty in feeding us.

He decided to head up north to Utica. He went to work laying railroad tracks and ties under the WPA program (Works Progress Administration), that was set up under Franklin Delano Roosevelt's New Deal; a way to promote work, due to the surging unemployment.

It was tough on Mom and Dad to be separated. She had two young children to look after, and was pregnant with her third.

Pete wrote a loving letter home telling Mom to take care of us and herself to make sure we were well. It was a valentine to her. The letter told about conditions upstate; there were a great deal of disreputable characters up there. He had no intention of allowing our family to even see the kind of sordid element he was forced to work with, which was why we were not allowed to visit. He sent all his money home to take care of his family, hating every minute of the separation, but always knowing his responsibilities.

He survived that time without incident because of an important *Peteism.* "If you don't like somebody or you think they are trouble, just walk away." He went on, "It takes more of a man to walk away, than to fight people who are not worth your effort." He had no intention of becoming anything like the men who were there.

His focus was on his family at home which led to this *Peteism:* "Take care of your family. A real man can be counted on. A man takes pride in himself, no matter what he has to do." He concluded, "If you are going to do something, do it well."

The crew manager told Pete that he was one of the best workers he ever had. Why doesn't that surprise me?

I have saved the letter showing Dad's concern for his family. You can see for yourself that he didn't have much to say, but the love he had for his family was simple, basic, and very strong. The spelling is indicative of the way Dad wrote. He spelled words exactly as they sound. I am *Babetes*, a nickname of some kind that Dad gave me when I was young.

Dad returned home from Utica in time to start the spring planting, hoping for a better year. The youngest child, Dominick,(Donnie) was born just thirteen months after me. He, like Elizabeth, the oldest, did not have much curiosity or desire to learn the customs of our grandparents. I guess a middle child reaches out more in every direction, so as not to feel left out. Who knows?

Dad made up his mind that he was never going to leave his family again. If necessary for survival, Pete would work two or three jobs, but always close to home, no matter what.

This is the letter:

Dear Kay

I received your letter and glad to hear from you and the kids Boy ol Sis the kids, I think at night how I yousto put them to bed and little Babeter how I yousto to play with him before he would go to sleep take good care of them and don't forget to get gabriel cod liver oil like we gave Elizebeth and get the cod liver oil for Elizebeth because it is good for them

it will prevent them from
catching a cold. I have no
money to sent you now
because you get paid every
15 days but as soon as I get
it I will sent it down to
you and you better go and
get your glasses & see a
doctor about that feaver
you get every night, don't
say yes and then forget all
about it let me know all
in the next letter, About
hear I don't like the city

it all gets full of the coal dust from the cotton milles and railroad it is something like pokepsey? In the camp hear they are only a bunch of bums you even get discusted to get near some of them. we are about 1 and a half mile from the City of Utica I don't like the place very mutch to have you and the kids up hear their isn't mutch work up hear it is hanging around this Bums

no more to say till
I hear from you and the
kids and the rest

Best Regards
to all
From your
loveing Husband

Pete

Dad continued to work the farm, concentrating at the beginning on selling produce that could be turned around quickly.

Summer seasons would be particularly lucrative for selling strawberries, blackberries, currants, cherries, and corn; actually he sold anything that would turn a quick buck. He fertilized and sprayed the trees that were starting to come along, working with Joe Gurga, our inherited help. Joe was with us for a large part of his life, helping out on the farm. He lived in our basement, near the boiler.

Joe was an orphan, born on the fourth of July, who lived with one family. Then, he was inherited by my grandfather, and then came into our lives where he spent 25 years. He would never sit at the table, although my mother wanted him to. He would rather sit on the steps leading up to the attic and eat his meals. He would tell us all kinds of stories. Most of them were imaginary, but we always showed him respect. It was just expected of us.

At the end of Joe's life, my mother's brother, also named Joe, put him in an assisted living home and let him live out his life there, taking care of the bills.

To make extra money, Dad worked odd jobs for other farmers, helping with their harvests, fixing their equipment, renting himself and his tractor out wherever necessary.

Dad repeated some thought provoking *Peteisms* that come from his life as a farmer. The first was a belief that all farmers share: "Whatever you sow will reap the harvest. That is the power of a seed. I have a right to a harvest as long as I do not take any shortcuts and do all the necessary things to reap the rewards." It sounds so simple, yet it is so powerful.

The other *Peteism* he instilled in me was a life lesson I have experienced many times, and I know Dad is whispering it in my ear every time I have to start over: "You do what you have to do to survive and provide for your family. Remember, when life gets you down on one knee, you still have another to get back up on."

My answer to him is simply this, "Amen."

As time went on, it was still a struggle. Mom and Dad were constantly thinking of new ways to make money, and came up with an idea. They would continue to work the farm, but would also open a luncheonette in Marlboro, right down the road on Route 9W, having noticed that many truckers went through the area every day. Mom was a great cook; she could make anything. Dad made the best pizza ever. They would use these talents to survive.

There was no area at the café for all three of us kids to play in. Elizabeth and Dom were content to just be with Mom and Dad; they knew their place and behaved. I, on the other hand, was one curious kid. I asked too many questions, talked to all the people coming in, a regular busybody. I tried to help with everything, from cooking to cleaning, to serving. I was still a baby, not yet five years old. Guess I must have inherited Pete's work ethic gene.

One day, for no particular reason, I decided to go for a walk outside the store onto the busy 9W highway. An eighteen wheeler was barreling down on me. My Uncle Steve was visiting. He dashed out of the store and snatched me off the road just in time. My mother fainted. My father didn't know whether to hug me or spank me. This incident changed the dynamics in the luncheonette and their desire to keep it waned.

I was sent off to my maternal grandparents every day after that while my parents worked. For me, this was not a punishment. I enjoyed being there anyway. Remember, I was king in that house and loved playing the role. My parents though, were not happy about putting an additional burden on Mom's parents; at least that's how they saw it. Of course, Mom's parents did not. All the same, a short time later, the luncheonette was sold.

Mom and Dad's sister, Bridgette

Gabriel 1 yr. old, with Elizabeth 4 yrs, old

Catherine Cicale on the caterpillar

Donnie and Gabriel on the tractor

Gabriel 3 yrs. Old, Donnie 2 yrs. old

Aunt Grace (Mom's sister) with Gabriel and Donnie

Peter and Catherine Cicale with children (1948)

Donnie, Dad and Gabriel

Chapter 12

GABRIEL RETURNS

In everything that was happening, lives moving so fast, no one talked about Gabriel. As a reminder, he high-tailed it out of town right after the funeral, never looking back. He returned to Italy, the old country, and stayed there for two years. He didn't contact any members of the family; no one tried to find him either. He had his agenda, and was working hard on continuing his laid-back lifestyle. At the time of Elizabetta's death, he was already an old man of 76 years. It was pointless to tell him that though. He had plans and they did not include dying. He went back to the same town he had come from, the place he had met Elizabetta.

His son, Michael, had married his first cousin Florence. She had a sister, Nunziata who had a daughter, Philomena, his niece. Incest ran in the family for many generations. So it was no surprise when Gabriel married this woman, who was 38 years younger than him. Her motive was to get to America; he had the money to make it happen. So, this mutually beneficial "love match" turned into marriage.

When Gabriel returned to America with his new wife, he bought a large home on the opposite side of the Hudson in Poughkeepsie, about four miles from the farm. He also bought a six family building, giving him income from the rental apartments. He was set to go on, family be damned.

He sired an additional child at the age of eighty-six, ten years later, making the front page of the Poughkeepsie News. He was photographed holding up his ten fingers, representing that he was now the proud father of his tenth child.

I was a teenager. Everyone in school asked me if I was related to the old man in the photo, Gabriel Cicale. I denied it, mortified that he had another child at that age.

As I've told you earlier, no one was allowed to say one bad word about my grandfather. None of us did, at least not in front of my father. Dad never felt sorry for himself. He never complained about the decision his father had made to sell the land out from under him. Dad believed in and taught us this lesson: "Honor the Ten Commandments. That means respect your mother and father. Family is family."

I am still not sure I get this in relation to Gabriel, but Dad was adamant about speaking disrespectfully about his father.

Our family went to visit him less than a half dozen times. My mother would come with us. The visits would be short. Gabriel, in keeping with his usual character, asked a few questions; but he never waited for an answer. Gabriel gave orders to Philomena just as he had done with his first wife. She jumped to fill his requests. Sound familiar? Their son, Pasquale, looks exactly like his father. There was no denying the familial resemblance.

When Gabriel was ninety-two and legally blind, he had a massive stroke. The doctors said the end was here. There was no sadness from the family this time; after all he had never shown any kindness to his family. Everyone was expecting – and I'm sure in some cases hoping for – an imminent death. The next morning Gabriel woke up as if nothing was wrong. He was just as tenacious as ever. He yelled to his wife in Italian, "Io famo." (I am hungry.)

What a surprise! He had a breakfast of freshly squeezed juice, homemade bread, eggs, sausage, pancakes, and coffee. Yep, ol' Gabriel was back to his ornery self.

He lasted another six years, finally dying at ninety-eight years of age. A major teaching hospital asked to study his organs. The family complied. The results were astonishing. They found that his organs were that of a fifty-year-old. Let's all start the Gabriel Cicale diet – a raw onion and a gallon of wine a day. We could probably live forever.

Dad had a lesson for us, in spite of the atrocious behavior shown him by his father. He wanted us to know that he believed in living life as his mother and our maternal grandparents led their lives.

The *Peteism* is short and on the money, "Live a respectful honorable life. This will be passed on to your children."

What a heavy burden to have been such a special child to a man who really did not deserve it. But this did not matter to my father. He had to live with himself. And he did it with absolute dignity.

Chapter 13

FAMILY LIFE

The next few years flew by. Life went on for the man who "didn't expect, so he wasn't disappointed." He just rolled up his sleeves a little farther and continued along his journey. Please don't misunderstand. Pete was not a simpleton, nor a weak man, he was just a man of quiet strength; a man who knew his role, and looked at the past as just that. If he ever felt down, he never showed it. He may have been more human than those who knew him thought, but we'll never know anything more based on his actions.

P.S. Before I forget, the entire book is built on information told to me by my mother. She was the only person he ever shared these stories with. Dad

NEVER talked about himself or his travails in life with anyone else.

Dad's unstoppable zest for life, love for family, and powerful drive to just work, gave him the impetus to continue to build his small farm. Luckily, working a parcel of land was something he really knew how to do well.

He kept himself busy plying his lifelong love for the soil. He went into the fields early in the morning, working into the night. His schedule remained as before. He came in for his hot lunch and went back to the fields, returning for dinner.

We were a family, a cohesive unit. We all were in our places at 5 PM for the evening meal. Dad took his place at the head of the table, casually sitting with his legs to the side, rather than under the table. He never sat with his feet squarely under a table, no matter where he was. I often wonder about this quirk. Unfortunately I never asked him, or if I had remembered to, he probably would not have had an explanation.

Meals were a time to come together. Dad did not say much, but when he did speak, it was always something that would help us, his children, through life. Of course we didn't always see it that way at the time. After dinner, Dad would take five or six apples. He ate three by himself. He would then cut the remaining apples in quarters and asked each one of us, "You want a piece of apple?"

I can't speak for my brother and sister, but I really did not want an apple slice because Dad did not peel it. "Dad, I don't like the skin," I would complain.

He did not listen. He was always pushing apples; it was our main crop. It was our dessert. "The skin is the best part, where you get your vitamins. Nothing bad can come from an apple," he'd say. It was that basic.

I remember that even when we were very young, we knew that dinner was a time for respect. We behaved. It was just expected of us. There was no such thing as not eating what was served, or questioning the choice that mom had made in preparing the meal. She was a great Italian cook. We were appreciative for what we had.

I do not remember hard times or a shortage of food during my youngest years. I may have been too young, but I do recall many sad meals as I grew older.

When I was ten years old, Dad ran out of money to feed the family. He had to think of something that he could afford. It also had to be filling. We were big kids who loved to eat.

As an aside, we all grew up to be quite tall; I am 6"4", my brother 6'3", my sister 5'9", very unusual for our generation of Italians. Think about it, most men of my generation, of all nationalities, grew to a maximum height of 5'10".

My mother was 5'6". Dominick, her father, was big at 5'10", her mother was 4'11", a little quiet religious woman. Mom ended up being the tallest girl in her family.

Of course, the giant of this information about height statistics in both families was my grandfather, Gabriel, who was 6'2", born in the late 1800s, more than very rare for that time, with his wife Elizabetta a few inches short of 5'3". My father was 5'10", becoming the tallest of all his siblings.

It must have been the farm life for all of us; but for Gabriel, who knows what made him grow so tall? If you visit Italy today, the average height for men over fifty is about 5'8"; probably due to lack of proper nutriments.

We were already getting eight gallons of milk delivered weekly. We did have a cow, but it did not provide enough milk for our growing bodies. When we had better financial years, we would have pigs, sheep, and even a steer that would be slaughtered for the meat, and kept in a freezer for the winter months.

We would bring our animals right up the road from our farm. The old barn that Mr. Quimby owned would act as a slaughterhouse, butchery, and a curing barn.

That barn was one of the most photographed barns on the east coast of New York. It would stand as a reminder of simpler times, until it finally collapsed from the deteriorating wood and aging of over one hundred years.

We also had the bread man coming weekly with six loaves. That was common in rural areas like Milton. We were active and hungry.

But during lean years, we did not have much to fall back on. I remember one winter when Dad had a dilemma and faced it head on.

He went to the local supermarket, Grand Union, to see what would work. Dad did all the food shopping for the family. First of all, Mom did not drive. She also could not go to a supermarket and just buy a few things, even though she was great with numbers. She had to walk down all the aisles and impulse buy, something Dad knew was a dangerous thing to do.

Dad knew the produce manager well. He walked up to Mike Stanton and said, "I'm going through a tough spell as far as feeding the kids, and if I could pick up some bananas, they would be filling, give the kids potassium, and get me through till some of my vegetable crop is ready."

Mike knew that it took a lot for Pete to speak like that, and replied, "I have about thirty pounds left before my shipment tomorrow morning that I could sell you."

"How much do you want?"

"I could give you all of them for six bucks."

"Mike, I only have three bucks."

"No problem that will work."

Dad came home with 30 lbs. of bananas, which would be served for all three meals, lasting about two weeks. We never complained. We ate bananas, and even tried to make some jokes at the table about it.

"Is this it?" I threw up my hands in mock amazement.

"Yeah that's it," Dad shrugged.

"What's for lunch?"

Expressionless, Dad said,. "Some delicious bananas,"

"Dinner?"

"Guess what? We have some wonderful bananas," Dad winked.

We ate bananas until they were gone and the money loosened up. You know what? I eat a banana every day, still love them, and I believe my dad's story that you need them for your daily potassium. I always tell people about the infamous banana saga, to show them how lucky we are to have whatever we have.

Dad instilled a work ethic in all of us at an early age; the same lessons he taught himself as a young boy on Pleasant Ave. in NYC. Dad taught us how to help work the farm.

At two years of age, he started bringing me out to the fields. Of course, I didn't do much, just watched him work. At that same age when I went to my grandparents' home, Dominick would also take me into the fields, put me on his lap on the tractor, and as I mentioned earlier, taught me how to maneuver the steering wheel. I could not reach the pedal or I might have been able to convince him that I should drive. Remember, I was "King Gabriel" at his home.

By the time I was four, I would pick up fallen branches or brush that would hamper my father from tilling the fields properly. I would add the biggest sticks to the wood pile to burn in the fireplace.

With each age, or growth spurt, I would start to do more and more. I never complained. I was being trained by the greatest worker ever.

By the time I was eight, after school and on weekends, I was driving the tractors out in the fields with Dad and Joe Gergu.

I would walk the field picking up fallen apples that were called drops. My father would sell those to the cider mills. Nothing would be wasted or left to rot on the farm. Everything that was grown had to be turned into money.

As I grew older, my workload became more intense. I helped till the fields, plant, harvest, work with the migrants when they came up for apple harvest, and helped in the packing house getting produce ready for sale, while my mother negotiated with the buyers.

When the apples were ready to pick there would be various buyers who would come up from NYC to purchase the crops of the local farmers. That occurred every season around the end of September, and my mother would do all the talking. A box would contain 40-42 pounds of apples depending on their size. For example, apples could be 2" around, 2¼" around, and all the way up to 3½" around. Of course, the larger the apples the fewer would fill each box.

When a buyer came in, Kate would give a price, such as "$2.50 and the box back." When the deal was accepted, it was done with a handshake. The box back was important, for it could be used the following year.

The crop would be sold to multiple buyers. If a buyer came after all the crop had been sold and tried to propose different terms that would be beneficial for our family – "I'll give you $2.75 and the box back" – you probably already know the answer.

Kate would say, "I already sold the entire crop." Even when a buyer pushed her, asking what she had sold it for, she would simply tell the truth.

"But Kate, I'm offering twenty-five cents more a box."

"The crop is already sold – done on a handshake. The Cicales do not go back on their word."

The transactions would entail many thousands of boxes when the harvest was fruitful. A quarter was a great deal of money and if that is multiplied by all the boxes, the extra cash would have helped us out; but she was Pete's wife and Dominick's daughter, names attached to honor in the Hudson Valley. She wanted to make sure that they stayed that way.

She had the same belief as Dad did in how to conduct business.

Using one of Dad's *Peteisms*, she said, "How you live life is the only lesson that counts. Never do to others what you would not want done to yourself. Your handshake and your word are all you need. If you have that you will never know that you do not have money. You'll feel like a millionaire, it's called Honor."

Mr. Quimby's barn

Chapter 14
A HAILSTORM

There came bumps and bigger bumps. Then came hills followed by mountains to climb for Pete.

The boy who had started with the shoeshine kit, graduating to the ice wagon, then to the laundry wagon and so many other menial jobs to provide for his family had adapted to any adversity that came his way. When the family moved to the farm, he taught himself to be a farmer. Was he successful at it? It depends on how you define success. He fed his family and took care of his responsibilities and obligations.

When Pete had his own family, he did what he had to do to survive. Remember, when his father threw him off the farm, he came through, didn't he? He knew from day one that the forty acres would not provide enough sustenance for all his children, now numbering three.

He had tried the luncheonette and realized with Mom that it was not the answer. He worked odd jobs for other farmers, helped in construction with Frankie, and still there was not enough money to make it through. He taught us to work with him, giving us more and more responsibility as we grew.

But, we were still young. I was only twelve years old in 1955 when life's hardships hit everyone in the Hudson Valley. It was not an exclusive Pete disaster. Rather, it hit the entire area of about 2,500 people. A severe hailstorm destroyed every farmer's crop. Towns faced devastation. Everyone was reeling. Like everybody else, Dad's crop was lost to the storm, coming just one week before the apples were going to be picked.

Dad knew that he could not meet his financial obligations to his family that year. He could not provide food for the table.

There was a company out of Pennsylvania that bought damaged crops like ours. Mrs. Smith sold pies in supermarkets. One of the representatives came to the Hudson Valley and bought all the damaged apples for use in pies. Dad sold the entire crop for one half of the value he would normally have received.

Government subsidies were in place for the farmers for catastrophic situations. It required tedious and intensive paperwork. The monies took a long time to filter down to the families in need, which would still not be enough to cover expenses.

Dad was a proud man, but he felt lost. He needed money to get the family through the rough winter. He would have to take care of next year's expenses, fertilizer, pesticides and all the other necessities for growing a new crop. He would then hope for the best for the following year, leaving it in the hands of God.

As an aside, a layman might think spraying crops is a simple process. It is not that easy at all. Farmers sprayed their crops often to prevent insects, fungicides, mites, anything that would hurt the crops. Whenever it rained, crops would have to be sprayed again, as the protection that was provided would have been washed off.

Mom, the financial arm of their team, sat Pete down to discuss how they were going to get through.

"Pete, we can't wait for the Federal subsidies. Even when the monies arrive, there will still not be enough to make it through to the next season. You need to see Joe at the bank."

"Kate, you know I don't like borrowing money. Besides, I have to get back to work."

"I am not asking you, Pete. I am telling you," she said emphatically, stepping out of her normal role in their relationship.

Pete relented and prepared to drive to the bank. He was dressed in his work clothes, having just come off the farm for lunch. "I'll go now and take Gabriel with me."

"Change first. You have a hole in your pants and you need to put on a clean shirt."

Pete stood his ground on this request. Dad was a simple man, a farmer. He did not want to clean up. "Do you really think he will loan me money based on what I wear? This is who I am. I am not changing."

Mom knew when to back off. She did not answer.

Dad called out to me, "Gabriel, come here. We have to go to the bank."

I asked, "what for?" I was always a nosy kid.

"Go with your father to see Joe Alfano, the bank president, Mom said testily. "Mind your manners and keep quiet. Do you understand?"

"Yes Mom, I get it," I replied, but I didn't really get it and wanted to know more.

We drove to the bank in Dad's 1949 Dodge half ton pickup. The truck chugged the three mile trip to the 1st National Bank of Highland. Dad was quiet. I knew enough not to say anything, just as Mom had warned me.

Joseph Alfano was looking out the window of his private office. He saw Dad come in. He came out to see how he could help him. Dad was not a steady visitor to the bank.

Dad started to explain his dilemma. "Joe, I don't know where to begin."

The president stopped him there. "Pete, let's go to my office for some privacy."

I, a young impressionable boy, was allowed to accompany Dad to Mr. Alfano's office and was witness to the conversation that followed.

Dad, with great humility and in simple terms explained, "Joe, I can't make it through the winter. I need a five thousand dollar loan to meet my obligations, feed my family, and plant next year's crop."

I watched as Dad choked on the last words, "I have nothing but my word to promise you that I will repay the money."

At that point, Joe walked over to Dad, put his arm on him and said, "I don't need to know anymore. Come with me Pete" and we followed him out of his office.

Joseph went to his assistant and told her, "Draw a check for Pete Cicale, the terms will be arranged at a later date."

"What do I have to sign?" Dad shook his head in disbelief.

"Nothing, the loan is being given because of who you are and who Dominick Porpiglia is. Now you take care of that fine lad of yours."

I smiled shyly.

He then turned to me. "Gabriel, I can't believe how tall you're getting. Remember to help your mom and dad. Okay?"

"Yes, Mr. Alfano, I promise," were the only words I muttered in the bank that day.

The loan was given on a handshake, the same kind of handshake that my Mom's dad gave the bank years earlier. The loan was given to Dad on his word, this simple honest man of character.

Dad paid back the loan with the next season's crop, all within a year. He promised himself that he would never humble himself in that way again, and until he died, he never did.

Dad was not really feeling good about himself at that moment, yet he knew a valuable lesson needed to be taught about what happened that day.

The *Peteism* I learned remains with me today. Part of this is a repeat of other lessons I had learned. But, he incorporated it into the day's importance as we drove back to the farm.

"Character and your name are all that we have in life. Be honorable, pay back your obligations, and be humble. Live your life prepared, and the rainy day savings will get you through. Son, when you are old enough to work full-time, save twenty-five cents of every dollar you earn. You never know when a rainy day will come, or you do not have work."

He had not been prepared, but he made sure that I saw what one has to do to get back on track. This message came from a proud man.

Pete took a second job in the graveyard shift at IBM as a machinist, working from eleven PM to seven AM, to get his family through the winter. It started as a simple solution, for it came with benefits like insurance and a pension. It ended up being a permanent supplement to the farm. Dad stayed with IBM for nineteen years until he was forced into retirement when he turned sixty-five.

It changed our lives slightly because it was a regular paycheck, not enough on its own to get us through, but a steady money stream nevertheless. How did Dad find time to sleep? I have no idea. When he was working the farm, he also worked at IBM. His first responsibility was to his family and that is just what he did.

Let me remind you that I was there that day at the bank and still did not learn that lesson until late in life.

You see many of us think that it will not happen to us, or that we can beat the system. You know what? I never found a magic short cut. Life has a way of bringing us back down to earth to face reality.

Chapter 15

FAMILY ROOTS

Life was difficult. I will forever remember that heartbreaking day at the bank when Dad had to ask for that loan. It was never discussed. To this day I do not know if my brother and sister were privy to what happened. We never had those kinds of conversations.

Dad said little anyways so why would he have discussed family problems? Instead he would turn his thoughts into his one-liners that would be our lessons from that experience. This *Peteism* says so much in a few words. "Respect those who say little and do much." He was a perfect example of this philosophy. "We should not talk just to hear ourselves."

He often reminded us at the dinner table, "The family will get us through if we stay true to our roots and remember who we are."

I did not always live up to that, but I should have.

We had a small television, but it had nothing to do with family time or dinner. TV was a very small part of our lives. Yes, it is true it was before the computer, and the cell phone, but people knew how to speak to one another, to entertain themselves, or play simple games like Monopoly or Charades around the table.

Life was not bleak. We had a lot to look forward to. Many weekends were shared with family and friends. Does anyone remember when it was fun and exciting to get together around a table with those that you love?

Holidays and family gatherings were not a time to dread, but rather a time to rejoice. They were the best times. We laughed at silly jokes and were teased, especially by Dad.

My mother's sister Angie and her husband, Uncle Steve, came often for weekends. It was always a holiday for everyone. They had no children of their own. They would arrive from Brooklyn with carloads of food, wine, liquor and toys for all the nieces and nephews. Oh, what fun. Everyone gathered at our home and the rest of the world and all our troubles would just vanish.

As I said earlier, Frankie had taught himself how to play many instruments.. Dad had a great singing voice. He would sing along to the music, harmonizing with his brother. Mom also had a beautiful voice. My sister sang well enough to perform on a musical stage if only Dad would have let her, but that is another story. I wasn't so bad either.

My uncles and aunts on both sides of the family loved to sing as well. There were Italian songs from past generations; hits of the day were also sung. *Pennies From Heaven, Heart of My Heart, Down By the Old Mill Stream, When Your Hair Has Turned to Silver, Oy Marie, Cela Luna* vibrated through the air as we all joined in, or simply clapped hands to the music.

We loved to laugh. When someone got started, it became contagious. We called it the "Cicale Jag." We laughed so hard and long that we forgot what we were laughing about. We were family and those were joyous times, no matter what the financial circumstances were at the moment.

I remember this *Peteism* whenever that little black cloud doesn't want to move on. "Laughing is a form of therapy that exercises your insides." I think of something funny and have a belly laugh.

Today some people have no idea what I am even talking about. Socializing with several generations is a thing that has disappeared in many families. The world has changed. Divorce has played a key role in breaking down the family structure. Moving to locations other than where we were born or grew up has also changed dynamics with our extended families.

We have lost the sense of family. However, if we go back to our roots and find "family," we can change how we view things.

We can redefine that word if we want to. How I view it is the way I see life today. A family could be a group not necessarily related by blood, rather by a sense of similar values, cores and elements, and a desire to bring back or start new traditions. We could laugh, sing, take walks outside, observe the beauty of the landscape, smile or say hello to people in the street. All these things cost ZERO.

It is up to us to realize that we have to be true to ourselves, care about others, and pay attention to what is happening around us. Then we can move forward, by going back to basics. Why would we want to do that? It is easy. Today's world may be more sophisticated, more technological, but it is a world of robots, people who cannot converse, or do not care about their fellow man. Children do not know how to play together or go outside to throw a ball.

Wouldn't that be a great way to bring ourselves back to earth?

1964
The Cicale siblings and spouses
Top Row: Peter, Frank, Mary, Mabel, Tony, Uncle Phil,
Louie and Mike
Bottom row: Catherine, Anna, Margaret,
Vincie, and Florence
Missing - Bettina, Bridgette

Chapter 16
FOLLOW THE RULES

Donnie egged me on. (His name is Dominick. I have always called him Donnie and it still drives him crazy. That's the breaks.)

"Bet you can't hit the windows of the chicken coop."

The coop was on the second story of the barn. Dad had taken two old windows and nailed them sideways on an opening he had made to give them light and air. We had 75 chickens for food and eggs.

I didn't think. I didn't take well to dares, especially from Donnie. We were only thirteen months apart, making us competitive in so many ways.

I laughed, "You got to be kidding. I could hit them with my eyes closed," and took aim with the gun. The pellets knocked out both windows.

What happened next, I hadn't planned on. I wasn't thinking about the repercussions, only showing off in front of Donnie. The chickens literally flew from the coop and took off running in all directions all over the fields. My father came running.

"What the hell did you two do?"

Donnie, the stool pigeon, stood grinning. He pointed at me. "Gabe did it, Dad." Thanks Donnie.

Dad grabbed the gun and told me to start running. I darted down the field and he shot me in the ass with the pellets.

"Ow! Ow! Dad that hurts," I yelled. I am lucky that is all he did.

"Now get back here, round up all these chickens, put them back where they belong and find a way to cover the holes so they don't escape. Understand? Get going now."

Donnie did help me gather up the chickens. I glared at him the whole time. We didn't talk for three days. But later we fixed it all up.

Did I deserve the punishment? You bet I did. But it could have been worse. Dad used a leather belt for other punishments. Do I think of it as corporal punishment? No. Honestly, it taught me some valuable lessons about the consequences of putting our family's livelihood in jeopardy.

Today, a child would call 911 and report a parent for abuse. I feel we have gone too far the other way to make everything politically correct. There must be some compromise to bring back parental discipline and family values to teach our children right from wrong.

I told you that the punishment depended on the crime. But, Dad never hit my sister, although in my opinion it would have been a good idea. She never did get the message that we were hurting financially. She wanted things that were really out of our family budget. Somehow, my mother always found a way to get her whatever she wanted. Am I resentful? No, of course I'm not. She was the only girl during a time when there was still a different set of expectations for each sex.

Dad was always looking for different ways to make money for the family, especially in between the apple crop planting or picking season. He sometimes sold produce. He'd buy large quantities from another farmer and mark it up to make a small profit.

One day he came home with a truck filled with watermelons of all different sizes. He had purchased them for fifty cents to a dollar each and was now going to sell them for one dollar fifty to two dollars.

After he arrived with the load, he stood beside the truck bed and called to me, "Gabriel, come here. Something is wrong."

I hurried on over to the truck.

"The farmer must have forgotten to put the watermelons in the center of the truck."

That gleam in his eye should have told me that something good was coming my way, but I never expected anything. That was what I was taught.

Dad then lifted a used bicycle from the truck, handing me the gift for my twelfth birthday and said, "Happy birthday son."

I was overjoyed. "Gee thanks, Dad."

That was it; there was no answer.

He never said much. His love as a father came through his deeds. That was the other side of him. Oh how I loved that bike, although by today's standards it would have been considered a piece of garbage.

I wanted to ride the bike. That was not going to happen at that time.

"Okay, enough of that," Dad said. "We have to get to work."

The bike celebration was over. Dad had a job for us. We were off to the Poughkeepsie projects on the other side of the river to sell the watermelons. We climbed into the truck and off we went.

"Watermelons for sale," Dad shouted from the truck. All the women would hear his yell and come hang out the windows of their small apartments.

"Hi Pete," they all grinned. Oh, they knew Pete.

He would flirt back, that smile gleaming in the sunlight. "Hi gorgeous, got some great watermelons for y'all."

The bargaining would begin.

"I'll take one, Pete."

"Cause you look so great today and you have all those kids, I'll give you a two-fer."

"Okay, Pete, thanks."

"No problem, sweetie. See ya next week."

Donnie and I delivered the produce to our customers. We were respectful, took the money, and turned it over to Dad. We didn't get paid. Dad couldn't afford to pay us. It was part of what was expected as our financial contribution to our family.

That day we heard this *Peteism*: "Take pride in yourself, no matter what you do. If you sell apples, watermelons, work in the field, it doesn't matter, as long as it is legal."

I was getting older. With that came more responsibility. At 14, I went to work in Gadaletto's Fish Market in Highland. I earned between thirty-five and fifty dollars a week. I worked after school and on Saturdays. Part of my job was figuring out how to get there. I hitchhiked to work and back home on a daily basis. There was always someone I knew who would pick me up. That was what small town living was like. Don't try that in today's world.

I brought my week's salary home to my mother. My Dad was proud of me, at least my mother said he was, for he never acknowledged that money. It was a given, just as he had done for his family by shining shoes or working on the laundry wagon.

Here is the *Peteism* my father taught me. "Work hard. Receive an honest day's pay for an honest day's work. Everybody has to carry his load. There is no free meal. There is no shortcutting the system. You work, you get paid. It's that simple."

I was a fairly decent athlete at school. I wanted to play sports and excelled at all of those I participated in. However, I had to work my practice and playing around a work schedule. I could play, but it could not interfere with my contribution to the family.

Dad was always working and never had the opportunity to watch me play. My mom had a scrapbook of all the sports articles written about me in the Poughkeepsie Journal. She would always tell Dad that I was in the newspaper again with accolades for my sports ability.

However, one night he decided to surprise me by attending a Friday night basketball game. He sat way up in the stands and watched me play. He did not understand the game or any of the other sports I participated in. He was too busy working to learn the rules of these leisure time activities.

It was only in his seventieth year of living that he started to watch television and learned the fundamentals of football and basketball so that he could converse with me about the professional games on television. Anyway, I digress.

Dad turned to the man sitting next to him that night and said, "Is my son any good?"

The man replied, "Your son is better than good, he is the team."

The team played hard but we lost by four points. I made three quarters of the points we scored.

At the end of the game I looked up to the stands. There in the top row stood Dad. He raised his hand, gave me a giant smile, and yelled, "Atta boy!"

I will have that moment inside me until the day I die.

In my late teens, I was expected to work the farm as I had always done, but now with more responsibility. I was bigger and stronger. I could ease some of the tremendous burden that Dad carried.

I knew my priorities as I was witness to the many sacrifices my father had made as we grew up. I remember a time when he was working in the field pruning trees. He had the tractor and the trailer attached. He had to get to a limb he missed pruning. He was on a slight hill. He jumped off the tractor and climbed onto the trailer to get to the height he needed to get at that branch. All of a sudden, the tractor started to roll. He had forgotten to put on the emergency brake. He jumped off the trailer and went to grab the brake, not realizing that the rear tire was about to roll over his ankle. That is exactly what happened.

We were all at school. He had no one to help him. With all his might, he yanked the brake handle. His foot was starting to swell. But he had work to do. He continued his chores for another six hours, though he was in excruciating pain. By the time he came out of the field his ankle had swollen to almost ten times its normal size.

My mother looked at him, and in a shrill nervous voice she shrieked, "What did you do?" She then fainted.

I was home by then. We attended to mom, calmed her a little, and then took Dad to the hospital.

He spent the next ten days there. His ankle was so enlarged that they could not put a cast on it until the swelling went down.

You already know that cast and all, he was back in the field the very day he was allowed to come home.

I knew how hard Dad worked and I wanted to help out as much as possible, but I was a teenager with raging hormones. I was dating; enjoying parties every Saturday night. I was expected to work in the field every Sunday morning. Dad often had to yell to wake me up.

One morning I just couldn't move. I had partied too much. This time Dad came to my room. He had yelled out for me once too often.

He picked me up and carried me out to the field. Now, I was no lightweight. I was bigger than my father. However, he had superhuman strength from a life of hard labor. Believe it or not, I was still sleeping. He dumped me in the field and walked back to his tractor. I still didn't move.

He had dropped me right in the middle of a trench he was digging. He used the bucket to dump dirt over me, then started for another load. That woke me up real fast and I was angry.

"What are you doing?" I shouted.

"Were you supposed to be out here this morning? Now, get up and start working."

He didn't care how tired I was.

This *Peteism* spouted out, "If you say you are going to work, that is a promise. A promise is to be kept. That is your word and your word has to mean something. Anyone can BS, and BS is dirt cheap."

In Dad's world, life was simple. You did what was expected of you. Maybe that was one of the secrets of his contentment with his lot in life.

I continued to push the envelope. Don't all kids?

The difference is that others were not the son of Pete Cicale. One night after hanging out with my best friend, Danny, we were exhausted. We both came into our house and tiptoed into my bedroom. I shared a room with Donnie, so I gave Danny a blanket and he instantly fell asleep on the floor. I did likewise in my bed.

Dad came home from his night shift at IBM. Following his nightly routine, he looked in on us before going to bed. He found Danny in our room.

Lights went on, not a norm for Dad. He disregarded his own *Peteism* due to the circumstances. ("Conserve energy, close doors, shut off lights, turn off water and tighten when not using it. Don't leave anything running.") But, that night was a different story.

"What are you doing here, Danny?"

I answered for him, "We were too tired. I couldn't drive him home."

"Did you ask permission?"

"No, Dad, I didn't."

"Sorry Danny – Out. We have rules in this house."

He took Danny's clothing and threw them out the front door.

It was freezing out and there was snow on the ground. I quickly threw something on and ran after Danny to drive him home. He was shivering to death and trying to get dressed as fast as he could go.

"Wow, I never want to mess with your ole man."

I knew Dad was right. Rules are rules and we had to obey them. In retrospect, it is great to know that as long I followed the rules, I could stay out of trouble on the home front.

I was expected to behave according to my lessons in life. My sister had different lessons, but just as firm. Elizabeth had a beautiful voice and loved to sing. She found a job singing at a club nearby. She was all excited, but did not tell Dad.

Somehow, he found out and went directly to that club. There was my sister singing in a smoke filled room. There was merry carousing: drinking, loud music blasting, wild dancing, and drunken laughter. My father walked straight to the stage, took Elizabeth by the hand, escorted her right to the car and drove her home. No daughter of his was going to be hanging out with unsavory people.

His lesson was clear, his *Peteism* for all his children. "Be careful about the people you hang out with. Remember, if you hang out with shit, you become shit. You hang out with people who are going places, you are going to go places or at least have a chance of going too."

Dad believed this with every fiber in his body. He was going to make sure that we turned out okay. That was his job as a parent. Singing in nightclubs was not his idea of a healthy lifestyle.

My sister was very embarrassed. But she learned that lesson the hard way. She never pushed in the wrong direction again. Dad was determined to put her on the right track. He planned his strategy.

He made up his mind that Elizabeth, who had excellent secretarial skills, was going to work at IBM. He wanted her to make a good salary and have good benefits.

My sister did not have Dad's work ethic or drive. All the same, this was his little girl, his favorite child, and he had to start her on the right path. Nothing against my brother and I, but this was his daughter. He was her protector.

For almost a year, Dad walked past the office of the President of IBM and spoke with his secretary. He asked for a job for my sister. He was religious in his determination. Every day he came back, and every day he reminded the secretary of his daughter. The president would watch him from the window of his office.

Finally, he asked his assistant why my Dad kept coming back each day. He was told that Dad was looking for a job for his daughter. The president asked his assistant to go to Human Resources and get my sister's file.

He said, "Any man who is that persistent must have a child who would work hard, if given the chance."

My sister was given that opportunity thanks to Dad. She was an outstanding employee of IBM for almost twenty years.

His *Peteism* wasn't 100% accurate as it pertained to Liz, but it was for the rest of us. He just became her surrogate in his determination to make things happen. "Nobody is going to do it for you unless you do it yourself. Don't wait for somebody to do it for you. You'll wait a long time. Whatever you want, you have to do it yourself."

He had made an exception for Elizabeth, but he never interfered in helping her again. He felt that he found her the job. Now she was on her own to use what he'd taught her.

Chapter 17

THE FAMILY GROWS

We grew up in Dad's world. He worked so hard and so long that sometimes he had no time to sleep. But he never complained. He just did the best he could on the farm and at IBM.

Dad drove whatever vehicle he had bought for the best price at that time. He never bought new trucks or cars. He bought what ran, period. When a truck or car finally gave out, only then did he look for a replacement.

I remember the *Peteism* he taught us. "Do not care what people think. Do not try to impress them with material things like your car. Be who you are, like it or not." He said, "Does the car get you from Point A to Point B? That is all that matters."

Jealousy of someone who had a better car or house or more money was not in his heart. When money issues were getting him down, he just improvised.

He figured that IBM had so many employees, why not use that to his advantage? He began arriving early for his shifts, his car packed with the produce of the season. Everyone knew Pete.

"Come get your fresh produce!" he would yell out, and the IBMers would crowd around.

Sometimes it was peaches, sometimes tomatoes, apples –anything that he had at the time.

"How much are you charging Pete?"

He'd shrug his shoulders. "Aw, we all work together. I don't want much."

He'd ask for a few bucks, depending on what he was selling. It was always less than the supermarket. It was also as fresh as could be, picked that day from the farm.

Everyone went home happy. Pete always sold out of whatever he had brought. I should say almost everyone was happy. For some reason, a few complaints went to the higher ups.

Pete was told, "Sorry, but you can't sell things in the parking lot on IBM property... regulations you know."

He simply replied, "Sorry about that," knowing he would be doing the same thing the next day. He knew he had to.

Truth be told, the same people who told him he had to stop were also some of his best customers. They looked the other way when he continued his little side business.

This was probably one of the most important *Peteisms* ever taught us:

"Nobody is going to look out for you, except you.

Nobody is going to feed you, except you.

Nobody is going to fight for you, except you.

Nobody is going to work as hard for you, as you.

Nobody is going to give you money, unless you earn it.

Instead of looking for something that is more than likely not going to come, do it yourself."

We were growing older and life changes were starting to happen. While a great athlete, I was considered a dummy in school, simply because I was not interested. I did not take academic courses. I was looking for the shortcut out of high school.

I knew Dad's *Peteism*, "the shortcut to success is hard work. A shortcut sometimes becomes a long cut when you try to cut corners, thinking you are smarter that the feat you are working on." I understood the message. I chose to ignore it.

I was too busy with girls and sports. I graduated 66th out of a class of 67. Bravo, that is a terrific accomplishment. Ha! I am emphasizing this for a reason. I graduated as a "Future Farmer of America". There is nothing wrong with going that route if you are going to be a farmer. But I had bigger dreams. I wanted off the farm and into the business world. I wanted the big money.

I went to work at anything that I could make a good buck at – mostly construction. It was manual labor. Dad was not happy. Yes, I was making money, but I was spending it, not thinking anything about the future. He let me know it every chance he got.

I was young and stupid. I dated a lot, bought cars that I dressed up to show off, everything that was the opposite of what Dad had taught me.

Dad started suffering from some serious health issues, all a result of his hard labor. He didn't complain, he just accepted whatever came his way. Mom was a strong advocate of preventive medicine, vitamins, etc. But even she could not prevent the ailments that caused his body to fail. First it was his back. I can't imagine why. He was operated on when he was fifty years old.

A very famous female neurosurgeon, Dr. Stimson performed the surgery. She had just finished performing surgery on Arthur Godfrey, a famous television star of the time.

Dad's roommate at Vassar Brothers Hospital was a fine young man, only twenty-six years old. During the few days before they were to have identical surgeries, the two developed a warm relationship. He was frightened. Dad never had fear. He convinced the young man that it would all work out okay. Dad's surgery came. The next day was the young man's. I do not remember his name but I do remember his sad fate. He became paralyzed. He talked about that young man for a long time afterwards. It bothered my father that something so irreversible could happen to someone so young, at the prime of his life

During that time, any surgery required weeks of hospital care and recuperation. Dad had to stay for three weeks. He would often bless IBM, for they paid 100% of the bill. Dad recovered quickly, defying the odds. The minute he could walk out of the hospital, he went back to work at both of his jobs. He worked with a body cast under his arms to the top of his genital area, fulfilling all his obligations with this cast on for six months.

After that surgery at fifty, for the rest of his life, Dad's body fought with his mind. Remember the tractor rolling over his leg? He also had gall bladder surgery, requiring a temporary colostomy. He continued working as if he were twenty.

My sister lived up to his expectations. He'd told her that you become who you hang out with. She met an IBMer, Jerry, a really smart guy; an engineer in the department where she was a secretary. And she married him. One down, two to go.

I was working construction after high school, making a good buck. I was satisfied and thought myself a big shot in town. After all, I had achieved some fame as a great athlete.

I met Joann. She had moved up from Queens. She had hated city life. She was very intelligent and had graduated high school at fifteen. She was going on with her education, studying to be a nurse at Vassar Brothers Hospital School of Nursing. I was a farm boy, a country hick. I thought that she was the ticket for me to acquire the sophistication of the city.

It was a difficult time in the United States. The Vietnam War was escalating. There was a lottery system in place at the time. If your number came in low when you turned eighteen, you were going to be drafted. My number was thirty-eight. I knew where I was going.

I wanted to get my service completed so I could go on with my life; I wanted my choice of services. I enlisted in the Navy before the Army called me. Off I went to the Great Lakes for boot camp, almost freezing to death during my basic training.

I remember a specific day in November 1963 as if it were yesterday. Eighty guys were in class; I was in Company 48. The instructor told all the recruits to walk to the window and look out. He said, "Gentlemen, look at the flagpole. You will notice that the ensign (a term used in the service for flag) is flying at half mast. Please be seated." With an enormous amount of trepidation, we took our seats.

"I am here to inform you that at 12:30PM Central Standard Time today, November 22, 1963 our beloved President, John Fitzgerald Kennedy was assassinated in Dallas Texas.

Everyone alive at that time remembers where they were. I was terrified. Were we at war? If so, who was the enemy? What would be the repercussions?

The base was shut down. For four long days we were glued to the television as the world watched the aftermath of that horrific day.

It turns out that I personally did not need to worry about what my role would be in the Navy. Shortly thereafter when we were having our final physicals before going overseas to Vietnam, the doctor discovered that I had an MCL in my left knee, and was not fit for service. I was sent home with an Honorable Discharge from the Armed Forces. My career was over.

Now, I could go on with my life under my own terms. First thing, I married Joann. Two down, one to go.

We moved into the basement of my parent's little house. It was fixed up for us, making things a little easier. I always told her that I had dreams. I always wanted to be a businessman in NYC. She had always wanted a country life. What is wrong with this picture? I'm sure you'll figure it out, but wait awhile.

Donnie was smart. He graduated high school, took a year off and then went back to school. He would graduate from Marist College in Poughkeepsie, New York. He met his future wife, Liz, at around the same time and took the plunge three years after me. Three down, none to go.

Dad had to have cortisone shots in his shoulders so that he could use his arms. Everything hurt. Dad was still working his two jobs.

Back to the hospital he went. He needed traction for his neck, a result of his earlier back surgery and the years of pain that he was enduring. His body was placed backwards on a hospital bed, with his head at the foot of the bed. They hooked Dad up to twelve pound weights to stretch his neck in an attempt to alleviate the pressure of a deteriorating disc.

Someone on staff opened a window to get air circulating in the room. That simple move led to a series of disasters. Dad caught a draft as the air temperature dropped rapidly that day. By the time my mother saw that Dad was shaking and closed the window, it was already too late.

He started going downhill very quickly. The chill led to a cold which quickly developed into pleurisy pneumonia. It worsened. His heart couldn't fight the infection and he developed pericarditis. Phlebitis came next. Dad was rushed to intensive care and an oxygen tent was put over him, from his head to his knees. He was critical. The doctors were not optimistic. None of us were prepared.

The priest came in to give Dad last rites.

I went to visit him daily. There was that giant oxygen tent covering him.

Dad motioned with his finger for me to move forward.

I pulled my chair up next to him. "What is it, Dad?"

He whispered to me, "Gabriel, come closer. I have to talk to you. I need you to promise me something."

"Dad, what do you need?" I was apprehensive about what he might ask me.

"Gabriel, you need to get an education. You need to go to college."

How was I going to do that? I didn't have any academic background. I had taken the easy way out of high school. My classes at Highland High were made up of Business Math, Shop, Farming skills, anything that would get me a diploma by just getting by. Heck, I had not taken any prerequisite math or science classes that could have prepared me for college.

"Dad, I can't do that. I am not smart enough."

"Gabriel, don't BS me. You are very smart. You are just lazy. Now promise me."

My father was dying. What could I do? "I promise Dad," not having the foggiest idea of how I could ever keep that promise.

Guess what? My father recovered and I had a promise to keep. He had no intention of dying. He was a fighter. He still had work to do and mouths to feed.

I looked at my wife.

She shrugged, "You made a promise. Now you have to keep it."

Chapter 18

I MADE A PROMISE

I registered at Ulster County Community College to try to make an easy transition into college life. I knew I was not ready for a four year institution. Besides, who would take me with my credentials? I started out at Ulster on a probationary status. I had a lot to prove if I intended to stay there. I was a fish out of water, but I had a promise to live up to. I started to put my head into the books.

I worked hard at school. Joann helped me study. I worked construction during the summers to help us financially. I worked nights as a bartender, anything, to make money. Little by little, I caught on and graduated with an AA degree.

In 1965 while I was on a mission to finish my education, Dad experienced the joy of having his first grandchild. Elizabeth had a son she named Gerald Glenn Walker IV. Obviously her husband was not Italian; but rather from a long line of G.G. Walkers. With a moniker like that he had to reach success in life. He would have no choice. The family was ecstatic. He was my godson. Dad embraced his new role, for now Pete had another generation to teach.

How he loved this child. Jerry must have felt that incredible unconditional love, for he later wrote his college application essay on his grandfather, his "Pop Pop."

Only his grandchildren were allowed to call him that. If anyone else called him "Pop", he would say, "I am not your Pop. Got it?"

Just so you know, Jerry lived up to that long name, becoming quite successful on Wall Street. Where else?

Our family was growing. I transferred to Marist College where Donnie was enrolled. He graduated ahead of me. He hadn't wasted time. He always knew he was going to college.

It was an expensive private school, now ranked one of the top 100 private colleges in the United States.

Joann worked there at the time as head of their new computer center and I was given a 25% discount as a result. She had paused in her nursing studies to help me. She was smart and could do so many things.

I made some great friends at college. We studied together, socialized, and saw each other through all of life's highs and lows.

One of my best friends for the remainder of his life was Daniel Coffey, to me one of the best people who ever lived. He raised a beautiful family of three boys with his wife Frannie. I think of him daily, he and his family are in my prayers. He was one of the people who perished on 9/11, as did his son Jason. What an American tragedy.

I became the first Honors Business Student in the history of Marist. Can you believe it?

It was a combination of my promise to Dad and this *Peteism*, "Your word has to mean something, so you can be counted on." I had followed his adage. He believed that a parent should "Give your children the tools that are important, so that when you are gone, they can survive on their own."

He did and I did.

When I graduated Marist, I was in the top 20% of the 450 members of our class. That was quite an achievement after my unremarkable high school placement.

Dad was at graduation, that infectious smile told me all I needed to know. He was all dressed up. He had even bought my mother an orchid corsage. She was as proud as a mother could be. I did it for "Pete's Sake," but I also did it for mine.

Dad used to say, "No one can ever take away your education."

You're so right Dad.

The following year, Dad turned sixty-five, the mandatory retirement age at IBM. He walked away sadly for he felt too young to be leaving.

His *Peteism* that relates to that job and everything else he has done in his life is, "Have pride in yourself, no matter what you do for a living, always do it well. Do it to the best of your ability."

He still had his pension. His health benefits were to serve him and my mother all the days of their lives.

Here is his *Peteism* relating to money and lifestyle: "Only use cash, if you have it you can spend it. If you don't have it, don't spend it. Only spend what you can afford. This will hopefully keep you out of debt." Dad also believed that "You should never make money your master.

Mom and Dad never used a credit card or ever went to an ATM. What happened to so many of us, especially me?

Gabriel, high school graduation

Gabriel, Navy boot camp

Mom and Dad
Gabriel's college graduation
Marist (1969)

Chapter 19

MARRIAGE

I believed I could now do anything and everything. That was exactly what I wanted to do with my life. I had fulfilled my promise to graduate college. Now, I could own the world.

My first job after graduation was beyond most peoples' wildest expectations. I was twenty-seven years old and making great money. The package for the job was $75,000 plus benefits. I was becoming what I had said I was going to be, a businessman.

How did I get this job? Milton was a small town. Red Prezziosi, a very shrewd businessman, was one of two self-made millionaires who lived there. When our family went to church every Sunday, Red always made a point of speaking with me. He loved my gift of gab. He told my mother when I was quite young that someday I was going to work for him. I kept that in the back of my mind.

After graduation, I approached Red about a job. He welcomed me into his company. I was hired to sell plastic bags for a territory from New York to Maine. I liked that. I felt important.

From the beginning, I was aggressive, assertive, and unafraid. Red totally believed in my ability. I immediately proved him right. I was great at what I did. It came so easy. I could sell anything, travel with the best of them, eat at the best places, Yes, I know, it was on an expense account. I didn't think of it that way. My head swelled rapidly.

I moved up the ladder quickly. I knew that I would someday take over his company. That was Red's plan.

Joann and I moved to a big Victorian house in Poughkeepsie. We had Peter in July 1970 and Daria came eighteen months later on Christmas Eve 1971.

Pop Pop and Nana were thrilled. They now had three grandchildren. They took the job of being grandparents very seriously. We would go over to their home for Sunday dinners. Mom cooked each week like it was a Christmas feast. Many times my sister came with her family. My brother and his wife, and aunts and uncles from both sides of the family joined us. We continued the family legacy, gathering together, laughing, and singing. A new generation had arrived. It was the American dream.

But, I didn't wait long to burst the bubble of my own doing. I was restless, impatient to climb the ladder of success. I didn't want to follow the traditional route of one step at a time. I wanted to leap four steps, skipping the middle two. I wanted it all and I wanted it yesterday.

All of Dad's *Peteisms* meant nothing when I finally had my hands on a big pile of bucks. What happened to "Money is a sign of strength as long as you know what to do with it?" OR "Remember the way you leave people, you may need them again?" OR "The shortcut to success is hard work?" He had said them often enough.

I had a minor argument with Red. We often locked horns. I didn't like taking orders. I did not heed any of Dad's lessons. I impetuously quit the job that Red had given me. I felt that I had more to offer the world. I hurt a man who had treated me like gold. Why? Who knows?

I left a position that eventually would have led me to the top to go absolutely nowhere. I suddenly was unemployed. I found myself with a wife, two small children, a large house, fiscal responsibilities, and no job. What was I thinking? Obviously, I wasn't thinking at all.

On my behalf, I did have my father's work ethic and knew I had to do something fast. I read an ad for a firm looking for a recruiting professional.

Since money was not coming down from the sky and landing into my pocket nor were people knocking down the door to hire the next "President of the World", I applied for and got my next job with an employment agency. The firm name was Ethan Allen.

I found myself at the bottom of the ladder for one hundred dollars a week draw. I was starting all over again. I was willing to put in the time. What else could I do? My family was furious. I was too cocky or frightened to care. I knew I had to work hard to achieve. I had no idea what I was doing. But I knew I had a family at home and they were counting on me. By this time I already knew I had made a mistake in leaving Red. But, there was no returning, I was too proud.

A *Peteism* I had learned growing up was a now a thorn in my side: "All you can do is learn from your mistakes. The only way to learn is through experience."

Okay Dad, I just got your message, or did I? A company contest was announced. I had been with Ethan Allen for just a few weeks. But I was brash. I stood up at that company meeting, introduced myself to all the other national recruiters and told them that I was going to win that contest. At the time of my bravado, I really didn't even know what I was saying or doing. But the competitive juices that flow through an athlete were still running through my veins. I guess I was trying to convince myself that I was as good as I thought I was.

I worked day and night, WON THE CONTEST, and with a young man's arrogance continued the climb to taking over my supervisor's position.

Each week, when we reached plateaus, gifts were presented to the person on top. I went wire to wire, always at the top of the heap. I won so many prizes in that contest that I gave many of them to my mother and father and other relatives. My mother loved being treated like a queen. My father was skeptical. He did not like all these in your face gifts.

"Are you saving for that rainy day, son? Are you humble? Are you preparing yourself? You have a family, you know."

"Don't worry, Dad, I have it all covered."

"Make sure you do. Understand, son?"

I shrugged, "Yeah Dad, I understand."

I set myself into high gear and decided to buy the franchise office. I went back to my roots, the lessons from my father, to work out a way to get the capital for the purchase. After all, I had the honor of my name.

I returned to the family bank and entered Joe Alfano's office, the president. You remember him, don't you? He is the man who gave my father money when we lost our crop, all done on a handshake.

"Joe, I need a loan to buy out the current franchiser at Ethan Allen," I spoke with conviction. "I need $50,000. You know I'll pay you back."

"I know you will, Gabriel. I'll do it the same way I did it for your father and grandfather. But, this is not $5,000. Be smart."

I walked out of the bank with an unsecured loan. I was cocky. See how easy it was because my father and my maternal grandfather had laid the foundation before me.

I had bought the franchise within five months of starting there. The franchise territory I purchased ran on both sides of the Hudson River, from Westchester county on the east to Rockland county on the west, all the way up to south of Albany. It took six more months for me to open two additional offices in my territory. Within a two year period I had thirty-five people working for me.

Now, I thought I had learned the lesson. "The shortcut to success is hard work." I led by example, putting in eighteen hour days, seven days a week.

I started to enjoy money and success. People now knew the farm kid. I brought in a back room person, and made him a partner. After all, I couldn't do everything.

Bob was someone I met through business. He was a numbers guy, making $11,000 a year. I wasn't thinking clearly. I thought I needed a partner to watch the back end of the office. He worked out of the Poughkeepsie office, a staple of my Ethan Allen franchise that had been around for many years. All I really needed was a bookkeeper. But in my haste to cover all bases, or at least in thinking I was covering them, I offered him a partnership and money he could only dream about. I thought that would make him loyal and appreciative.

I told Dad. He frowned and this *Peteism* came from him. "Never trust anybody in business but yourself. You have no friends there."

I sighed. I thought I knew more than my father. What a jerk I was.

"Be careful, son. All you need is one bad apple. Within two weeks the whole basket will rot. What do you know about this guy?"

"Bob is a great guy. Besides, I can't do everything myself."

He tugged on his earlobe, deep in thought. Remember, Dad was born intuitive. He was the ultimate survivalist. "Okay, but make sure you get two signatures on every check."

"Sure Dad," I humored him.

I was the front of the operation. What did my father know about growing a company?

I was a salesman, so strong and dynamic; I thought that keeping my hands in all the pots would slow me down.

I kept building and now I was spending money to impress others.

Another of my father's *Peteism* came back into play. Am I saving twenty-five cents of every dollar I am now making? Of course, I was not.

The only thing I had insisted that Bob do was to pay the banker every week. Otherwise, I never looked at the books.

I kept at him and after some time I said, "Bob, did you pay off Joe Alfano?

"Sure Gabe, we're doing great. We even have a profit of $150,000 put away."

"Great, that's what I want to hear."

That was all I needed to know. Bob told me Joe was paid off. I had kept my word.

Bob was rewarded. He was now making about $150,000 a year, plus a car, plus benefits. Not bad for someone who a few years earlier was making $11K. I was happy for him, happier for myself.

As for the rest, I was too busy spending and building my own glory that I ignored the fundamentals taught me by the main man, Dad, who had truly experienced life.

At that time my Dad was not what I considered to be a great success. I was weighing his value in monetary terms only. How wrong I was.

I went to lunch every day, spent a fortune impressing the local clientele in Newburgh, New York where my first office was located. Newburgh was twelve miles south of my little town of Milton. It was a fairly large city, giant in comparison to Milton.

All the businessmen now knew Gabe Cicale. They saw someone who was a workaholic. They gave me all their business. I promised to fill their orders and delivered every time. Soon I had more business than I knew what to do with.

Chapter 20

SURPRISE

That is when stupidity really hit. I started to ignore the business, enjoying myself too much, spending freely, all things my father found to be offensive and too arrogant. I was being shortsighted, not looking toward long range goals.

I even ignored my family. I was never home. Times were changing. Divorce was starting to erode the family in our country. I felt that I had made a mistake in marrying young. I could not look forward to thirty or forty or more years married and tied down. I knew that I had to leave my wife, even though I had small children who would suffer the ramifications of such an act.

It didn't help when I came to my parents wanting to join the masses. "Mom, Dad, I am leaving Joann.

We want different things out of life. I don't want to grow old and regret not moving on."

"What does that mean?" my mother spoke sharply. "You have two babies at home. Peter is only two and a half and Daria is one. Have you lost your mind?"

"I want to be happy and haven't been for a very long time."

Dad said little. His face said it all. His usual smile was no longer there.

I tried to avoid his stare. That wasn't going to happen.

He said, "Let's go for a walk."

I followed him outside, somewhat begrudgingly.

The only time my father ever spoke about the divorce was that time. "You know you took a vow, son. Your mother and I have been married a long time. There were storms along the way. Life was not always a picnic. We each could have left. But we knew that was not even an option. A vow is a vow."

"But Dad, should I just stay and be miserable for the rest of my life? I will take care of my children. I promise you."

"Then this conversation is over. You are still my son."

We walked silently back to the house.

My mother wasn't finished. She was harsh. "We don't divorce in this family. No one has ever divorced. What will I tell everyone?"

"Tell them the truth, Mom," and I left the house.

A wrench was put into the relationship with my mother for quite some time. She was worried about the children. She sided with Joann. Close relatives stopped speaking to me. It was a mess.

To add insult to injury, my brother-in-law Jerry thought this opened the door for him to do likewise, and he left Elizabeth two weeks later.

Now there were three grandchildren in the family who would be growing up in broken homes.

What could I say? I thought of the words of my father, "If you could lay your head on the pillow at night and get a good night's sleep when the room has no one but yourself in it, then you will know that you have done the right thing. If not, you will have to live with your actions, live with yourself." I knew that a piece of me would always be reminded of that *Peteism*.

But I could not live in my marriage. I felt that my dad's generation was not mine. The divorce went through.

Chapter 21

SELF ABSORBED

I was divorced, free to do what I wanted to. And I wanted it all.

I had big dreams. I had to make more money. The divorce cost plenty. Yes, I was making good bucks, but I had obligations. I needed more. I promised to help Joann get her nursing degree. What a sport. Was that all I owed her?

I thought of that $150,000 profit that Bob had told me about. I wanted to expand my horizons, spread my wings into other businesses. For I was again impetuous, not thinking of my father's lessons.

I wanted to buy an outside business, a Carroll's franchise; later that company was to become part of the Burger King organization.

"We have no money for that kind of investment," Bob said. "We're one hundred and fifty thousand dollars in the RED."

Fire came out of my head. My blood pressure must have hit the roof.

"Where did the money go? Where is our profit?" I screamed.

He just looked at me and muttered, "You know nothing about bookkeeping."

I steamed out of the Poughkeepsie office that day, called a dear friend, a mentor of mine. Al was a very famous lawyer. He put me in touch with two business lawyers. I went to see both of them. They told me that I had a hard case to prove. There could be two sets of books. I had no way of knowing and it would cost a fortune to prove what had really happened to our business. Both lawyers suggested the same thing.

I followed their instructions. I cut my losses in order to get rid of the bad apple. I sat down with Bob and gave him the Poughkeepsie office; thus, breaking the partnership.

My father had warned me that that you have no friends in business. I will never know what happened to that money. But I have a good idea. My inside partner, Bob, and our accountant were great buddies. I will leave it at that.

My father had said "Get checks requiring two signatures." I had not listened to that either. Now I had to pay the piper. Where was my savings? I had none, I was too busy spending. I had to reach out to save my business. I needed $25,000 to keep going and to meet payroll.

I went back to Joe Alfano, my banker. He had given me the initial seed money to buy into the company and start my business. He had given me that money with only a handshake, based on HONOR. Now, I needed more money to stay afloat.

Joe put his arm around me. "Gabriel, times have changed. I need you to fill out some paperwork and I need to present it to the Board of Directors."

The arrogant farm boy came back to play. I lost control. "Who, me? Why? I never needed that the last time. You got all your money back, didn't you?"

"Banking is evolving, Gabriel. That is the new bank policy."

"Well then, the hell with you. I don't need you," the words came spewing out of my big mouth.

Always dignified, Joe calmly responded, "You're going to regret speaking to me in that tone."

I left in a huff. The very next day he cut off my credit line.

My business was crumbling, for I had forgotten to continue with my father's basic lessons. I had stopped working, stopped leading by example, and stopped watching my own business. I let others run my business as I tried to reap the harvest of something that had not grown properly, without the right nutrients.

So now my father's other lesson came to fruition, one of the people on the board of that bank was Red.

Oh shit! I remembered how I had treated him when he was so good to me. I found out later on that he was one of the vetoes in not giving me that second loan. Did I deserve for that to happen? You bet I did.

I had mistreated Joe Alfano by speaking disrespectfully. Many years later, after being humbled in life, I apologized to my banker for my arrogance. He forgave me. After all, I am still my father's son.

I saved the business with my parents' help, something I deeply regret. They took out a second mortgage on their home. My father did not want to do it. He didn't owe a dime and at his age he didn't want to start having any debt. My mother drove him crazy until he did.

If Dad felt any additional burdens from what was happening with me, my business, or my divorce, he did not show it. He continued his farming but the aches and pains that came with his growing older were wearing on him. Did he complain? Of course he didn't.

Dad had added responsibility to pay off the second mortgage I had talked him into. He worked the farm as hard as he ever had. He was selling fruit to the projects. He still showed up at IBM between shifts peddling produce from his car to catch a few bucks. They always let him in. Retired or not, Pete was one of them. They loved him.

I was slowly paying him back. He had worked an arrangement with the bank to pay them monthly, or rather my mother did.

I felt guilty. I was still spending. I saw things I wanted or thought I needed them for much of my life. I had not learned the lessons of my Dad. I needed new luxury cars, expensive clothing, a House Beautiful home with designer furnishings, and dining in four-star restaurants. Did I learn this from my Dad? NO, he did his best to instill in me the belief that our value system comes from within.

A *Peteism* came forth, "If you have pride in yourself, you will never know that you do not have money."

Why couldn't I get that? I tried to buy my way through life. A simple farm hick had made it and wanted everyone to know that. I bought my parents new furniture, appliances, carpeting, lamps, silver.

My father was angry, "Didn't you learn anything? Put that money away. We don't need anything."

Why didn't I just repay the loan to them at a faster pace? I guess it was because I thought my streak would never end. I liked showing off, the antithesis of my father.

Two years later he decided to sell the farm. He kept five acres of land for himself. He didn't like being closed in. He still remembered those tenement days. He was sixty-eight years old and had no desire to retire. He simply could not handle the responsibilities of full time farming.

What did he do? He worked for other farmers. He was a foreman during apple picking time. There was no one better. He'd tie up grape vines, making them more productive. He was a jack of all trades. The people of the Hudson Valley knew him, respected him, and knew he could be counted on. He was never without work. The second mortgage was paid off through the fruit of his labor.

It all worked out in the end. My sister inherited the house. My brother was given an acre of the land to build a house on. I did not return all the money I had borrowed, only about seventy-five percent, due to changes in my life. But, that was another story. I expected and received nothing more. I shot my load when I borrowed the money from them.

Dad found an ad in the local Milton paper for a Park Superintendent. It was only from Memorial Day to Labor Day each year. He applied and was awarded the job.

Now, he was in his own heaven. He was back to the soil and was surrounded by all the beauty of the land. He had concessions to oversee, boat rentals, landscaping. Everything he loved was right there in his job. The best part was that everyone knew and loved him, old and young alike.

"Hi Pete," was reverberated every day.

The beaming smile appeared all over that handsome man; still the same look he had as a young man. The years of labor gave him that tanned leathery look, miles of white hair would greet you, "Hi yourself, have a great day."

He was at peace.

Chapter 22

REALITY

The *Peteisms* were right in front of me. They could have easily banged me on the head. "Don't make money your master. If it is not in your pocket, don't spend it. Be thankful for little things. Do not live life unaware. Always be prepared."

Did I practice any of this? NO, I had a "testa dura" (hard head).

Inevitably, I lost control of my own business. I was having too much fun to listen to Dad. Actually I was having too much fun to listen to anyone. I was hobnobbing with the elite of the area, although I should not have been. I was "keeping up with the biggest Joneses around." Idiot!

I was forced to sell the business. I had to admit defeat.

I stayed in the area for awhile because of my kids. I turned down two fantastic opportunities that required relocation due to guilt about leaving my children.

I bought a small bar in Poughkeepsie; named it Gabe's Place and made a good buck there. But like all things that came too easy to me, I got restless. I didn't like the long hours. When I was in the bar I would sing, entertain, and schmooze with my customers.

The clientele was an entirely different element. These were working class people, the salt of the earth. But, like all bars, fights broke out. People overstayed their welcome and I had to send them home. I even had one person stabbed to death in front of the joint.

I did well, so well that I started to slack off again. I hired a young aggressive kid to be my manager. He seemed hungry enough. The only problem was that my manager thought he was my partner. The monies coming in were less than a third of what I had been bringing in.

Guess I still hadn't learned. Is this starting to sound redundant? I hadn't recorded any *Peteisms*. I closed the bar, turned in the liquor license and decided to move on.

I no longer felt good inside when I bumped into people in the area. I decided if I really wanted to make big bucks again, I had to move into New York City. I knew I had a responsibility to pay for my children, and the big money was elsewhere. I moved right outside Manhattan to New Jersey.

I was now living in a different state. I thought it was close enough to see the kids often, although I was probably lying to myself. I went back into the recruitment field and started making big money again,

When I had my kids for visitation weekends, we always stopped in to see my parents. My mother had forgiven me a long time before. In fact, in accord with the values that my father and mother lived by, she apologized to me for not defending me to the family after the divorce. That was something she did not have to do.

I tried to stay close to my children. I now lived one and a half hours away. I came up every other weekend. When they were very young, I was clueless as to what to do with them. How many men know how to entertain or care for infants?

As time went on, I planned outings and vacations, always trying to make up for my leaving. I bought them clothing, paid for furniture, played ball with them, took them to sporting events, even taking them to upscale restaurants; anything to make them happy. At least, I thought I was making them happy. I still hadn't learned the values that my father had tried to teach me. We don't have to "buy for the sake of buying."

All my children wanted were love and consistency. I know it now, better late than never.

My father and mother lived approximately ten miles away from my children. When I was not able to be around for my children, my parents filled in for me.

Dad took over by leading through example. He did for my children more than most grandparents would do. He taught them his values. "Family will always be there. When it is all said and done, family has to stick together." He spent quality time with my children. He had them work the small land that he still owned behind the house.

If snowstorms came to the Hudson Valley, even though he was in his seventies, Dad would drive the ten miles over treacherous roads to where my children lived. He would shovel their driveway, providing a path for Peter and Daria to walk to the bus. He knew that they could then get to school.

If he felt the weather was too bad, he'd drive them to school. He nurtured them in a way that he could never have done for me. He simply did not have the time when I was young.

Dad repeated the lessons for them. The *Peteisms* flowed. He had changed slightly in his feelings about girls. If you remember, there was a time when he yanked my sister off the stage in a nightclub where she was singing.

Well, when my daughter came around, the only granddaughter, he became involved in feminine equality. He called her "Champ", told her that she could do anything a boy could do, probably better. That part of her character has to have come from Dad. She is a strong independent woman today.

He put up a swing in the cherry tree behind our house where they climbed as high as they wanted to. They picked so many some times, that they would get stomach aches. They collected apples, planted fruits and vegetables, picked and packed them.

Dad even had time to play horseshoes and catch with me and the kids, something he could never have done when I was young – always too much work to do.

My children grew to be great athletes in the Hudson Valley, especially Peter who could fill several rooms with trophies from his swimming achievements. Dad watched them compete in swimming, rooting them on. My kids absolutely loved their grandparents.

Peter later became the second best swimmer in the back stroke in the United States. He was widely recruited for college.

At age 75, Dad had to come face-to-face with another major health issue. He had colon cancer. My mother read everything available on taking care of him.

Joann, my ex-wife, was now a nurse at Vassar Brothers Hospital. She had remained close to my parents. She made sure Dad was taken care of.

221

The surgery went well. The doctor was confident he had removed all of it. After two follow-up visits, Dad was given a clean bill of health. He was told to return in five years, to check him again.

In retrospect, a doctor should never have allowed a cancer patient to wait five years before checking him again. But, that is another issue.

Dad, 68 yrs. Old with Donnie and Mom
He never cared how he dressed

(1983) Christmas, Mom and Dad kissing

Pete at 75 years of age

Nana and Pop Pop Cicale, Gabriel, Daria, and Peter Cicale

Pete with grandchildren, Jerry, Daria and Peter 1975

Pop Pop at 75 years old with Daria

Jerry, Peter, Pop Pop, and Daria

Chapter 23

IN THE PARK

Father and son continued to sit quietly in the park. It was Labor Day weekend, the day before the park would close until next summer.

The comfortable silence that had ensued all afternoon spoke volumes about their relationship. Dad did not speak unless he felt he had something to say. While he was smiling to himself reminiscing about his almost eight decades of life, I had much deeper thoughts.

Pete was a loner in life. He was a man of rarified air, inhaled by very few. How many of us live life in true contentment? He was able to be by himself for hours on end.

Sitting sideways on the bench, his legs crossed, was the position most familiar to me. The late afternoon shadows outlined his still handsome face and curly white mane of hair. He certainly did not look seventy-nine years old. His body was in perfect proportion. He had the same toned appearance of a man in his twenties. His muscular five foot ten inches, his lean one hundred seventy-five pounds with a thirty-four inch waist looked better with each passing year. His sinewy arms and physique reflected his power; his entire look defied the ticking clock.

Maybe working eighteen hour days, seven days a week was the answer to not only longevity, but the fountain of youth? I thought to myself, *Maybe I need to go back on the cod liver oil and wheat germ of my youth?*

I chuckled to myself, Will I age like that? Will I have that movie star look? The wrinkled skin looking like it was painted perfectly to match his whole persona. I didn't take a second to think about it, *Nah, I doubt it.*

I didn't have to wait too long to see Dad in action. An attractive woman walked by. Her name was Helena, she was from the neighborhood.

"Hi Pete," she smiled. "Have a good winter. See you around." Helena was about forty-five years old and she was coming on to my father.

"Dad, Helena was just flirting with you."

"What are you talking about?" Dad was oblivious to people admiring him. He was a naive charmer.

I let it drop, but I couldn't help thinking once again about my mom. She would always point out women ogling my father. She would say to him, "It's not fair. You're getting better looking as you age. I'm just getting old."

Dad would say, "Kay, what are you worried about? I'm here, right?" He would then break into a rendition of *When Your Hair Has Turned to Silver*, his eyes gleaming.

She would shrug her shoulders, but inwardly loved the attention he was giving her.

Dad turned to me, waking me from my thoughts. "Are you at peace, son? Worried about something? It is all over your face."

"I'm fine, Dad. How are you feeling?"

"No problems. You know that. I just get the feeling that you're growing older, not wiser. Are you sure you're remembering all I taught you?"

"Yeah, Dad, I remember everything."

"Listen, I know you have responsibilities, but you're one person. You can only rely on yourself to get things done. If you expect others to do it for you, then you're a fool, and I didn't raise a fool."

That was a small part of the wheelbarrow full of *Peteisms* all spoken at once. I sat there absorbing that speech. Dad usually didn't speak that much all at once.

He continued, "You see all this, son?" He gestured with his hand. "Remember what I told you. It's a piece of heaven that God gave me to take care of, just like the farm. God is in the soil, right?"

I looked around, as if opening my eyes to the land for the first time, trying to visualize what my father was talking about. I grew up with this bountiful beauty all around me, the shining sky, the mountains behind us, the babbling brooks, the small lake of the park, with the canoes and rowboats on the shore, the trees on fire with the early Autumn hue; the smells of the country air, so fresh and clean, why had I never observed it closely before? I was always running away from all this.

"You're right Dad, I didn't forget."

I was about to speak further, but Dad had that faraway glaze in his eyes again. He was off somewhere in his world. Rather than disturb his thoughts, I went back into my world and there was silence again.

Dad was recalling the times that Red and Bill Palladino, the two millionaires who lived in Milton, had sought him out in the park to talk with. They both asked him the same thing in different ways on two separate occasions.

Pete remembered going home to Kate after Red came by, not really comprehending why he who appeared to have everything would have come to him. He had told his wife that he had asked him for the key to his contentment.

"Did he insult me, Kate? Was he making fun of me?"

"What did you say?" Mom said.

I asked him, "Why are you coming to me? You have all that you could want in life."

"And what did he say?"

"Kate, he told me he wasn't happy. He was worried about getting older. He was worried about his business. He was worried about dying."

"Pete," Mom answered, "he hasn't lived your life. He knows you have had your hardships. But you accept life, you rejoice in it, you love the days, you love the earth, you love your family, you love God. How many people have that kind of contentment?"

"Kate, I am nothing special. I simply don't expect anything. I told him, 'Don't expect and you'll never be disappointed.'"

"Well Pete, the world doesn't understand how you do that. Red wants to be like you. He just doesn't know how. He does not have your peace of mind. It doesn't matter that he has more material things than you. You don't care. You always look so happy, so joyful. He is not comfortable in his own skin. You have overcome everything, while he feels defeated. He envies you, is lonely, even among his own family. He has no children; He feels unloved."

Pete laughed to himself, remembering the second experience with the other millionaire. Bill Palladino had also come for the same answers. Pete still didn't get it. Bill had the world monetarily and children to boot. What was he trying to figure out?

He had come home to Kate. She had listened to him. She had seen his anguish.

"Why did they come to me, Kate? Are they talking to each other about me?" They came to me to learn how to live life. Don't you think it's a little late for them at this point?"

"Pete, it is never too late to get the message."

"Yeah Kay, I guess you're right. Ain't it sad?"

"It is. Think how lucky you are."

While Dad was in his world, I was praying that all was okay with him. My Aunt Gracie had told me that Dad had come to her the week before. He had asked her to take care of Mom if anything should happen to him. Why had he said that? He wasn't sick, was he?

I was afraid to bring up Aunt Gracie. Dad was my pillar. My mother and father were the glue that kept us together.

Pete's army rode up on their bikes. There were three boys about eleven years old. Every year, Pete had his little assistants who helped collect park fees, bring boats and canoes to shore that may have drifted, and other minor chores, driving around the park each day reporting back to Pete any problems.

One of the little guys spoke up, "Hey Pete, everything is done."

"Thanks, men. See you in the morning. Have a good night."

"You too Pete."

They were his pals. They loved the man. They rode off happy.

We sat comfortably for a while longer. It started to get dark. I knew I had a long trip home.

I broke the silence, speaking in barely a whisper, "Dad, I'm heading out. Don't worry about me."

We kissed each other. I held him tightly, something a little out of character. But, today was a very reflective day for me. I wanted him to feel it too.

"I love you, Dad."

"I love you too," and he walked back into the park to do his final check, to make sure all the sheds and concessions were locked for the night.

I stood awhile, my eyes following his motion, until he was out of sight. Then I turned away and headed for my car.

Chapter 24

MY HERO

It was the winter of Dad's seventy-ninth year. He was still working as hard as he did his entire life. But Mom wanted him to ease up a little bit.

She spoke with Dr. Piccione. "I want Pete to take it easier. He doesn't want to. What should I do?"

Dr. Piccione, who was so much a part of our family simply replied, "Kate, on the day your husband slows down, he will be a very sick man."

Mom stopped in her tracks. She ended her conversation about Dad letting up.

Dad did slow down on his own in the Spring of 1985. He casually remarked to Mom, "I shouldn't say anything, but for the last few months I have a little pain in my stomach."

Mom went ballistic. Dad never complained about pain. By that afternoon, they were at the doctor. The complaints were quite real and he was immediately sent to the hospital. Dad's cancer was back. By the time he had all the tests run, it was too late. The cancer had metastasized to his liver and into his bloodstream.

Dad did not want chemotherapy. He made that quite clear to my mother. He didn't last long. That virile man went from working around the clock, to needing help getting to a chair, to not being able to walk or catch his breath. All this happened within three months. He had to be in excruciating pain. Still he never complained. On August 12, 1985, one month after his eightieth birthday, that incredible man was gone.

He died as he lived, with dignity.

Right before the funeral began, my daughter, Daria, who was thirteen at the time, came up to me and said, "Dad, I want to be a pallbearer for Pop Pop. Peter and Jerry are. What about me?"

"I cannot answer that. You have to talk with Nana."

My mother was old school. "Girls are not pallbearers. It's not correct."

"If Pop Pop was asked," she said defiantly, "he would have said sure. I was his champ, and he told me I could do anything that a boy could do."

I told her to sit down. This was not a day to have a confrontation with my mother. She sulked and went to her seat but reminded me about it afterwards, "It's not fair. Pop Pop would have wanted me to do it."

I told you she was strong.

At the beginning of our story I said that even during his last rites, Pete had no regrets What I did not tell you is that the wake and the funeral brought people from all walks of life, all ages, all friends of "Simply Pete."

Even the priest who gave him last rites at the hospital showed up at the funeral to honor this humble man. It was at St. James Church in Milton, our family church.

The funeral procession detoured on the way to the cemetery. All the cars drove into the town park, and passed through and out again, in honor of the man who had taken such good care of it.

Pete Cicale is resting in peace. Of that I am sure.

He is happy.

PS. Mom was only sixty-eight when Dad died. It was only after Dad died that she finally had surgery to correct her eyesight. I remember her looking at me afterwards, softly touching my face, "That's what you look like. I never really saw how handsome you really are."

I grinned from ear-to-ear, realizing how she must have overcompensated for her severe handicap for almost seven decades. I teased her, "You should have seen how handsome Dad was. All the women were crazy about him."

She never really recovered. She lived one day short of her eighty-ninth birthday. Her last twelve years were spent in an Alzheimer's unit. When I came to visit, I could always bring her back to me.

I would walk down the hallway and before entering her room, I would start to serenade her just like Dad did with melodies of their time and Italian songs. *When Your Hair Has Turned to Silver* would resonate through the halls and from her room would come the next line in her beautiful lilting voice, "I will love you just the same."

I'd enter the room and she'd be smiling. We would then spend several hours singing, laughing, and reminiscing about the good old days as if she had no problems with her memory. It was only at the very end that I couldn't bring her back anymore.

I pray that you, my readers, have the love and role models similar to my parents. If you don't, I have just shared them with you. They would not mind at all if you borrowed them.

Chapter 25

EPILOGUE THE REASON

As I have suggested throughout this story, this is a universal wake-up call. That is why I felt this book needed to be written. I lived life exactly like many others are. I saw things I wanted or thought I needed for much of my life. I had not learned the valuable lessons from my Dad. I had to have all the material things many people probably want. Did I learn any of that from Dad? NO, he tried to instill in me the belief that our value system comes from within. Now the question is, are you living life as I did, or do you already know Pete's lessons?

Why couldn't I get that? Dad always knew that there were bigger houses, bigger cars, and fancy restaurants. My humble father never measured his worth through others. He did not care. Life is really in how we see it. Should we really care what others think or feel or do?

Our society tries to reinforce what we should have daily on television, on the Net, Facebook, Twitter, and certain books and movies. Are we all guilty of having fallen into it? We probably are. Most of us have spent too much, and have joined the masses with credit card debt, bought houses and cars we could not afford. What did we accomplish?

The family is falling apart or has already fallen apart.

This *Peteism* is a reminder of that problem:

"Your family is like a branch of a tree. If it cracks or breaks off, you may hurt the chance of the tree surviving."

Dad is looking down on all of us smiling that famous grin that won over everyone he met, and I can hear him saying, "Didn't I tell you this was going to happen? Did you save your money? Here is that rainy day."

Pete Cicale was not an ordinary man. I invite you to learn his lessons well and stick with them for the rest of your lives. In that way you will always be rich inside. Finally, if you believe that people are born to learn and if they do, they don't return again, then you have learned all of life's lessons. Pete *wouldn't* be back again. I hope we all can learn from his *Peteisms*.

If I can save you from my mistakes in life, then I have accomplished a promise I made to myself. Spare yourself the pain.

Dad, thanks for the lessons. I learned a lot and found out I needed to use them not just some of the time, but always...

And to my Readers: May you find Dad's peace of mind.

PETEISMS

I am listing some of Dad's lessons. They are not all original. Some may have been in your family for years. I have tried to include most of them throughout his life story. But I couldn't possibly relay all of them. To follow are those I remember, along with my wish that you are able to use them well.

- ★ Spend only what you have in your pocket. Don't spend what you have to borrow.

- ★ Don't make money your master, be the king of your cash.

- ★ Money is a sign of strength, as long as you know what to do with it.

★ Save twenty-five cents of every dollar you earn. You never know when a rainy day will come, or you do not have work.

★ Your family is like a branch of a tree. If it cracks or breaks off, you may hurt the chance of the tree surviving.

★ If you have pride, you will never know that you don't have money.

★ The most important person in your world is named Bill, dollar Bill. When you have him in your life, you have lots of friends. When you don't have him, let me see who your friends are.

★ Get what you pay for. Anybody can buy retail. The smart man will shop and buy wholesale. That extra money you save goes in your pocket.
If it is going into someone's pocket; it might as well be yours.

★ Don't get impressed with yourself or others, as to what you see. What you don't see (character) is what is important. In other words, believe all you actually see and none of what you hear (gossip).

★ Respect those who say little and do a lot.

★ Your word has to mean something so you can be counted upon.

★ If you think you can do a job but have insecurity about it, take the job anyway, because the job is going to go to someone. Why not you?

★ Laughing is a form of therapy. It is a way of exercising your insides.

★ Be thankful for little things. You may be waiting a long time for the big ones that may never come.

★ Have pride in yourself, no matter what you do for a living; always do it well no matter what. Do it to the best of your ability.

★ Don't expect anything to just come to you. Just do your job. The rest will take care of itself.

★ Never do to others what you would not want done to yourself. Your handshake and your word are all you need. If you have that, you will never know that you do not have money. You'll feel like a millionaire, it is called honor.

★ A shortcut sometimes becomes a long cut when you try to cut corners, thinking you are smarter than the feat you are working on.

★ Who you hang out with is generally who and what you become.

★ People have short memories, Example: what have you done for me lately?

★ Pace Yourself.
Life is like a creeper gear on a tractor. Go slow and learn from your mistakes. As you learn, increase your gear.
If you go too fast, you will miss what is around you.
Going a little bit slower will allow you to learn and see it correctly.

★ Don't always want what you don't have. If you think the grass looks greener on the other side of the fence, look closer. You will see that there are brown spots and holes there, just like on your side of the fence.

★ People will be jealous of you when you get a promotion. Remember, there are no friends in business.

★ If you take away a man's place to go when he gets up in the morning, you take away a man's reason to get up.

★ When you listen closely, people are telling you what they want from you. When it is your turn to talk, you just have to give them back their own words, and you probably will be giving them the answer.

★ If you don't expect, you'll never be disappointed.

★ If you don't like somebody, simply walk away.

★ Life is made up of simple working parts.
Go do what you have to Get enough sleep and have time to spend on what you want to do.
You will do the most with the limited amount of time you have.

★ The shortest shortcut to success is hard work.

★ God is in the soil.
Make sure you take time to get in touch with it.
Feel it with your hands.
Know God is present in the soil you have in your hands.

★ Give your children the tools that are important, so that when you are gone, they can survive on their own.

★ You are given more than one shot at success. In fact, you are given many. If you fail, try again. You must be willing to put in the time.

★ Stay grounded, always come back to center. When you were born, you were grounded, live the same way and you will die living a fulfilled life.

★ Nobody is going to look out for you except you.
Nobody is going to feed you, except you.
Nobody is going to work for you, except you.
Nobody is going to fight for you, except you.
Nobody is going to give you money, unless you earn it.

★ Do not care what other people think of you. Do not try to impress them with your clothes, car or whatever.
Be who you are, like it or not.

★ You can count your friends on one hand. In life, you will meet a lot of acquaintances, but you will have only one or two close friends who will be there no matter what.

★ Surround yourself with shit, you become shit. Surround yourself with people who are going places and maybe you might go places too.

★ Look at people's eyes when they talk to you. If they are looking away or not directly at you, they are not listening to what you have to say.

★ Shake a person's hand. If he has a strong handshake, it usually means he has strong character. If it is weak, it shows that he may be a soft wishy-washy person.

★ The most important thing in life is common sense. I'll take common sense over education any day of the week. If you are book smart, with no common sense, you might not be able to take what life throws at you.

★ How you live life is the only lesson in the end.

★ Live like a pauper and you'll become a millionaire.

★ People have short memories. They only remember what they want to. They probably will go back to their old ways where bigger is better. That is where they start to spend more than they have. It is called "keeping up with the Joneses."

★ Don't expect to be thanked for what you do. Do it because you want to. If a thank you comes your way, it is a bonus.

★ Remember when life gets you down on one knee; you still have another to get back up on.

★ If it looks cheap, there is something wrong, it probably is cheaply made. Buy less, but buy good. It will last.

★ All you can do is learn from your mistakes. The only way you learn is through experience.

★ Anybody can win by cheating, but to play it straight, be honest and win, that is a true winner.

★ Take heed of the way you leave people, you may be seeing them again.

★ You can always judge a man by the shine on his shoes. If I see a man with a clean suit and dirty shoes, I can tell that this person doesn't feel good inside.

★ Keep your mouth shut. Your actions are what counts in the end

★ If you do the right thing, then you can lay your head on the pillow at night, turn out the lights and get a good night's sleep, when no one is in the room but you. If not, you have to take a good hard look at yourself and what you are doing.

★ What is a hero? A hero is a guy or gal who lived a clean honest life, free of trouble, kept his name clean for his eventual son or daughter.

★ Don't get your heart set on one thing. It leaves you open for disappointment. There will always be another, guaranteed.

★ Life is made up of simple working parts.
Forward gear – do what you have to
Neutral gear – Sleep
Reverse gear – pleasure to spend with your family after providing for them, doing the most with the limited amount of parts you have.

A FINAL NOTE

Peter Cicale did not make up all of his *Peteisms*; they came from his family, his heritage, and people he met during his life. You, the reader, have similar lessons, passed down from your parents, grandparents; or those you have simply applied to your own life. We are a global society and all children of the world have learned from someone before them.

Please send me your lessons, so we can share and learn from them. If you wish, include your name, nationality or religion, ethnicity, anything you want us to know so that readers can visualize where your lessons came from. We can correlate them and pass them on to others through my website at www.petessakewisdom.com. We can also share our thoughts through my blog and twitter accounts, or I can be reached directly at ninacicale@aol.com. We can include your name or you may remain anonymous. The only thing I ask is that you send a way that we can contact you for authenticity and final approval before displaying them.

Until we meet again,

Nina Cicale

ABOUT THE AUTHOR

Nina Cicale was born and raised in New York. After graduation from Queens College, with a Masters in Education, writing was always part of her life, albeit not her professional career.

She was a teacher in the New York City education system. She also was an entrepreneur in the IT industry. She was a fundraiser for the University Of Miami School Of Medicine where she was awarded the honor of being chosen "Woman of the Year" for her humanitarian efforts.

She has been a ghost writer for several books, and also a writer of various motivational speeches. She has written poetry but has chosen not to have them published. Instead, with her husband Gabriel's impetus she has finally fulfilled her dream, to complete this book.

She lives in Palm Harbor, Florida with her husband, and dog, Chloe. You can visit her website at www.petessakewisdom.com.

1223

Made in the USA
Lexington, KY
20 November 2012